The Voice of Victory

One Man's Journey to Freedom
Through Healing and Forgiveness

By

Wayne Messmer

waynemessmer.com
Chicago

Wayne Messmer

WPM PRODUCTIONS, Inc.

The Voice of Victory, written and read by
Wayne Messmer

Song of Survival

-- The Daily Herald

A friend is one who knows the song in my heart and sings it to me when my memory fails.

-- Anonymous

Fans Roar in Tribute to Messmer

-- The Chicago Sun-Times

"And the Star Spangled Banner in triumph shall wave. O'er the land of the free and the home of the brave"
-- Francis Scott Key

Dedication

This book is dedicated to:
Kathleen, my wife and the love of my life
The proud memory of great parents
My Family

Dr. Seth Krosner, along with the other doctors and nurses at Cook County Hospital and Northwestern Memorial Hospital and Chicago Fire Department Paramedics Henry Hugel and Bill Steiner, whose expertise and commitment to their profession, saved my life

And

The millions of fans throughout the years who afforded me the privilege to lead them in the singing of the proudest of all songs, our National Anthem

Wayne Messmer

Contents

Stadium Singer Messmer Shot; Voice Imperiled

-- The Chicago Tribune

*"Our greatest glory is not in ever failing,
but in rising every time we fail"*
-- Confucius

Anthem Singer Messmer Shot In West Side Attack

--The Chicago Sun-Times

"Never, never, never, never quit."
--Winston Churchill

Cubs, Hawks vocalist shot in apparent robbery

--The Daily Herald

"Whether you think you can, or think you can't you are usually right."
--Henry Ford

Chapter 1

Introduction

December 1999 -- Chicago

This is a story of faith. It is a story of a great gift that was given, shared, stolen and returned to share again. It is a message of hope and optimism, built upon my will to live and the need to share the God-given gift of my singing voice with others.

Despite the overwhelming odds against me, I reached down and found the courage and conviction to fight through the obstacles of a devastating tragedy to return to life with passion and determination. Because of my faith, I also found a new appreciation of family and friends in the process of living life to the fullest, despite the inevitable interruptions.

My main message that I hope to impart in the narrative that follows is one of forgiveness. Despite the physical and emotional pain I suffered, I reached out to my assailants with compassion and truth and I came to the understanding that we are all God's children and we remain His children in spite of the poor choices we often make. Anyone who has ever been victimized, traumatized or in any way compromised should know that the ability to forgive is inside all of us. The question is how you deal with your own trauma and how you can find your own way to forgiveness. Anger and resentment are heavy burdens to carry.

These feelings hold us back from growing as people and prevent us from developing new and potentially rewarding relationships with others. Imagine looking at the person who, under oath in a court of law, told a judge and jury that he pulled the trigger of a gun with the intent to kill you. Most people will never find themselves in such an uncomfortable and anxious setting. Yet, in our daily lives, we all face our own attackers. Perhaps they don't attack us physically, but the intent to harm is there.

In my case, I had to accept the fact that the young man who shot me made his decision based upon his life experiences and the attitudes he brought with him to that very moment when he acted on his impulse. There is no excuse for his actions and there should be no dismissal of responsibility. Yet, justice was not mine to distribute. Forgiveness was my only intelligent choice. The bumper sticker making the claim that guns don't shoot people, people do, is partially true. The fact is that people with guns shoot people.

In my tragic incident, the gun itself did not overtake the person or the moment. The shooting occurred as a result of an individual having little or no regard for my life. This allowed him to pull the trigger of a high-powered handgun at point-blank range. The action came as easily as one pushes the button on a TV remote. In retrospect, the ease with which the attack took place is what saddens me the most.

The good news is that this is a story with a happy ending. We know that from the onset. My hope is that with this personal narrative, you will see that often we must lose something that is valuable to us in order to truly discover its worth. This story is the account of how I found the strength to rise up from adversity to meet my own challenges. Everyone's personal challenges are different, but we all must face what life hands us, however unfortunate and however unexpected.

In my journey, I was blessed to have knowledge of who I was and what I was all about prior to the incident. This story covers a span of two decades of remarkable opportunities, many of which provided great nourishment and enrichment both to my life and hopefully to the lives of others. It is a message beyond personal triumph and accomplishments, disappointments and tragedy.

This story is about the detailed account of working through the serious challenge of being forced to change. It is a diary of feelings, thoughts and emotions gathered from a lifetime of experience. The experiences described are my own unique life experiences, yet they may strike a familiar chord to others. My own story illustrates the unpredictable turns our lives often take.

This is a journey of both tremendous joy and sorrow. The story describes how I coped with the full spectrum of these emotions. Every day, each of us is constantly presented with challenges, whether it is closing a million-dollar business deal or just getting out of bed. Some challenges we welcome and embrace, others – often life-changing – are thrust at us at unsuspecting times and in unexpected ways.

One thing I have learned throughout the different phases of my ordeal is this: our character is not measured by the severity of the tragedies we face, but by our reaction to them. In our personal, spiritual, professional and family lives, we must constantly pray to be able to have the strength to clear the hurdles as they appear on the path before us, regardless of how insurmountable they may appear at first glance.

In the time since this drama first unfolded, I have had countless opportunities to tell this story and to touch the lives of other people. As a professional speaker, I have come to recognize that this signature story carries with it a responsibility. The strength I am able to draw from an audience is rivaled only by the energy they send back to me as

I carry the message across the country. Each of us have faced adversity in one form or another. It has become my primary mission in life to make a connection with people who need to hear a story of hope. This hope needs then to be translated into their own lives.

As my speaking career continues to grow, I have come to think of myself and my vocation as that of a professional encourager. A title with which I am quite pleased to be associated. In small gatherings or national conferences, the message remains basically the same. It is quite simply the story of my experiences during a horribly traumatic incident and my reaction to it. My story is true and, armed with the truth, we will be able to overcome any challenge that might arise.

Peace,

Wayne Messmer

Chicago, Illinois

Messmer Shooting Has Cubs Stunned
--The Daily Herald

*"I am not afraid of storms for I am learning
how to sail my ship."*
--Louisa May Alcott

15-Year-Old Boy Charged In Announcer's Shooting

--The Chicago Sun-Times

"Nothing in life is to be feared.
It is only to be understood."
--Marie Sklowdowska Curie

Chapter 2

The Verdict

The jury returned the verdict in less than two hours. The sound of the court clerk reading the words left me with a cold and empty feeling. There was no great joy or celebration, no immediate closure. Instead, the realization of what had just transpired left me with a million thoughts of what might have been on that fateful night three years earlier. My heart sank. It was a moment that I will never forget.

My wife sat there in the gallery for every minute of the proceedings. She watched as the dynamics of the trial unfolded. She bore witness to the arguments and the cross examinations as the jury heard the story of my life's most unforgettable moment.

As a witness for the prosecution, I had not been allowed in the courtroom to witness the trial as it was in progress. My time was spent in the law library upstairs where I waited anxiously; first to be summoned to testify and then again on this day of the final arguments when the jury had reached its unanimous decision. There had been the endless repetition of the facts, the little details of time, location, lighting, sounds and, certainly, the sights from my recollection that added up to no more than a brief flash in time. It was truly a surreal experience.

Everything that was being presented was related to about 15 unforgettable minutes in my life, minutes which were nearly my last. This snapshot of horror had been played out in my mind time and time again. I knew certain facts to be positively accurate. I recalled with unwavering detail the face of the person I saw that night as I approached my car on Chicago's West Side. Now, here in this courtroom, that face was within my sight. It was the very person whose image left and indelible impression on my memory as I fought to choose life during those crucial first moments after being shot.

My hands trembled as I stood motionless in one of the crowded benches behind the glass wall separating the spectators from the principal players in this courtroom drama. I stood in breathless silence and anticipation awaiting the decision of the twelve jurors who were told the story of an innocent, unsuspecting man returning to his car, only to be accosted, shot at close range and dismissed as an object rather than a person once the handgun had been fired.

I reached deep inside, grasping for an appropriate emotion. Will the jury respond to the impassioned arguments of the Cook County Assistant State's Attorneys assigned to prosecute the case? Did the panel of a dozen of my peers recognize the pain that was inflicted as a result of the actions carried out by the defendant and his accomplice? To me, the answers were obvious. The truth could not be silenced. Yet, waiting there to hear the verdict was a very uneasy time.

The words rang out in the Cook County Courtroom, "Guilty on the charge of attempted armed robbery. Guilty on the charge of attempted aggravated battery with a firearm. Lastly, and most significantly, guilty on the charge of attempted first-degree murder."

I remember having being disappointed by the failure of the justice system once before in this case and had lost a great deal of confidence in the process as a result. It was hard to accept the memory of another day in the not too distant past when I stood in Juvenile Court and heard the dismissal of the case against the young man who had confessed to pulling the trigger. He had managed to slip through the cracks of the system and had emerged from an endless series of appeals with the advantage of being tried as a juvenile for the cowardly act of which he had been accused.

The robbery attempt had not succeeded and I had survived the attack. Ironically, these were the two facts that served to work in his favor. The court system rallied to protect this young criminal, with a judge from the juvenile system leading the way, by intervening the process to block the upgrade of the case from juvenile court to the criminal court. I couldn't help but feel that disallowing the upgrade was a refusal to acknowledge the fact that this cold and heartless individual, whose premeditated attack that nearly cost me my life, was actually enjoying the benefits of a judicial system loophole.

I painfully recalled waiting for the Juvenile Court hearing, discovering that the prosecutor was essentially going to request a dismissal of the case against the young man who had shot me. I remembered the confusion I had to deal with in trying to bring myself to the point of understanding what was going on. The prosecutor informed me that this individual who had actually shot me and who had already been tried, convicted and sentenced to 12 years as an adult for an armed robbery committed on the same night as my attack, would serve his imposed time in the juvenile system until his 21st birthday, if my case, still classified as a juvenile crime, was left on his record.

In other words, I was being asked to consider going along with a plan with the State of Illinois to request that the juvenile case against him for trying to kill me be dismissed for time served. I was told that if I were to agree with the proposal, upon reaching the age of 18, he would then be placed in an adult facility to serve the remainder of his time of the armed robbery conviction, which had nothing to do with me. Should the juvenile matter remain on his record, he would spend his entire period of incarceration until age 21 in a juvenile facility, which was considered a much softer sentence. This would only happen if I agreed with the suggestion by the State's Attorney's office to essentially let him off the hook for shooting me.

I was sickened and dumbfounded by the situation. "Where was the fairness and justice in this scenario?" I asked. I could taste the disappointment in the system as I sat with Kathleen in the small room adjoining the juvenile court where the hearing was about to occur. What could I do? What could I say at that point? My feelings were that I had been victimized twice. Once by the perpetrator and now by the so-called justice system in which I had placed my hope.

Despite the efforts of the State's Attorney's Office to try the shooter as an adult, the case against him was left to be dealt with as a minor charge against whom the sympathetic judge, who had blocked the upgrade from juvenile to criminal status described as a "misguided and disadvantaged youth." My spirit had been uplifted only by the presence of the presiding judge in the Juvenile Court who had shared in my disgust with the situation and told the young man standing before his bench that he was not getting away with anything. The judge's words were stern and harsh.

He dismissed the case with the flair of a man who had seen far too many similar young criminals appear before him without remorse. His presence commanded attention and respect, which he demanded and received. If there was even a slight consolation, I had felt that at least one person in the justice system had at least acknowledged the insanity of this almost ridiculous drama that was unfolding before me.

It was this unsatisfactory conclusion to the case against my principal assailant why I felt the system had let me down before. I prayed that the case which was now to be concluded would help me to regain my confidence in the

13

existence of a balanced scale of justice. Ironically, it was my attacker — a now 18-year-old — that took the stand to detail the chilling account of the night of my greatest fear. He spoke in unwavering and unemotional tones about "how" he and his cohorts staged the evil plot of their night of crime.

This was a scene into which I had just happened to wander, unknowingly casting myself into the starring role. The details of the night flashed through my mind like a strobe, catching brief images of the facts and the faces as they had been recounted time and time again in the just completed trial. The central figure, now, was the young man who had faced the jury over the past few days. It was the same young man whom I had seen that memorable night.

The 16-year-old had returned that weekend to Chicago from Kentucky where he was attending high school and living with his uncle. Like many other kids across the city, he was a young man coming home for spring break. It was early April; the weather was just starting to turn, and the sense of excitement was in the air. Also like many other young men, he was filled with anticipation of the future. He had been sent to Louisville to escape the vicious street environment that he was about to become a part of this very evening. There was something in the air that night, something that spawned the need to be wild. The anticipation of the hunt — and possibly the kill — were too powerful to ignore.

He ran into the young accomplice who was armed and dangerous and who didn't want his feelings of power to go to waste. The would-be shooter was barely five feet five inches tall, yet his newly assigned position within a street gang and the gun he was carrying made him feel much bigger. He had been in trouble with the law many times before. He was comfortable and familiar with doing crime on the streets.

Prowling the streets of the west side neighborhood, looking for victims to satisfy his carnivorous appetite filled the moments leading up to my attack. He wanted to do stickups, and nothing was going to stop him. Nor would he allow anyone to tell him what to do, not even the sixteen-year-old – a year older and considerably wiser neighborhood youth – whom he had known since early childhood.

The scheme was not drafted in terms of exactness. The plans were not drawn with attention to detail of timing, location, best chance of not getting caught, et cetera. It was to be spontaneously acted out if and when the opportunity came up.

The area where it all occurred has seen its own evolution over the past 25 to 30 years, since it was known as the Old Neighborhood. It was, at one time, a community where the aroma of Mama Luigi's spaghetti sauce would waft about through the open and unlocked screen doors of the odd and even numbered houses along West Taylor Street. The personality of the neighborhood had drastically changed and from the perspective of three teenagers, neighborhood youths, the biggest change was yet to come... the change in each of their own lives as a result of some bad choices they would make in a matter of hours.

As they stood on Fillmore Street, they probably gave no thought to the fact that they were about to make a life-altering mistake. They most assuredly did not consider getting caught, tried, convicted and sentenced. They were too smart for that. Besides, they were only one hundred feet or so from the safety of their front doors. What could possibly go wrong?

A suburban hockey fan approached his parked car and the plan sprung into action. He had just spent some time at a bar/restaurant named Hawkeyes, a popular after-game gathering spot for Blackhawks fans. It was the same location where I was still enjoying the last moments of conversation before taking the identical trip on foot back to my own car.

The now courageous 15-year-old, energized by his weapon, stuck the gun to the neck of the unsuspecting victim, who obliged the gunman's request and handed over his wallet. Now, suddenly cast in the role of victim, the man emptied his pocket of the $40 in cash that he was carrying and since that was the extent of his valuables, he was happy to hand it over if it would only satisfy the armed robber and remove him from the wrong end of a barrel of a gun, the very same weapon which would play a crucial role in the night's drama not long after.

After he emptied his pockets, the gunman kicked him in the seat of his pants and took off on foot. Another youth who had worked the job of lookout in the caper also joined him. It was even easier than they had thought it would be. No resistance, no fight, no problem. They were drunk with the excitement of what they had just done. The best part was that the night was still young. There were certain to be more opportunities, more victims-in-waiting.

After splitting up the take, the trio of teens traded in the cash for snacks at an all-night convenience store. It was all too simple. The hunger for more was only temporarily subdued. Before long, it was time to strike again.

After being disappointed with the lack of substantial foot traffic from the local bars and restaurants, one of them called it quits. He had netted the least amount from the holdup and he had seen enough for the night. He walked home leaving the other two young men to their uncharted plans.

The 15-year-old with the gun had changed in the more than two years since the older teen had known him as the "funny little guy that he used to slap around like a little brother." He had since made the choice to associate with a gang. His status had been elevated after he had been attacked by a rival gang and severely beaten. Times were different now. He had a purpose, a mission and a hunger for crime.

Taking advantage of the fact that the housing complex was a short block from the patron's parking lot for Hawkeye's Bar and Grill, it was almost too convenient to pass up the chance for a quick stickup. Hawkeye's was a popular spot for the Blackhawks hockey crowd. It was a place where fans would stop before or after the game to get ready to cheer or to recount the game. Hawks players would often frequent the place along with a cheerful group of fans and, occasionally, me – the Guy who sings the Anthem.

The stickup technique was not sophisticated. It relied on the element of surprise. A person would come by en route to their car, a gun would be produced, and the cash would be handed over. It was as simple as that. All they needed was the next victim.

Earlier that night, I had been to the hockey game where the Blackhawks had defeated the St. Louis Blues 6-1 before a customarily enthusiastic crowd. It was a Friday night, a time when many in the crowd decided to let loose, have a few drinks and have a good time, thinking of the weekend ahead.

It was unusual in the fact that the Hawks generally played their home games on Wednesday and Sunday nights, so Friday was a good reason to celebrate, along with the victory still fresh in everyone's mind. Of course, with Spring just around the corner, it seemed as though everyone that particular night was in a good mood.

I had arrived at Hawkeye's shortly past 11:00 p.m., took my customary walk through the establishment to see the familiar faces and possibly talk to some fans. It was always fun to meet and greet the same folks who had hollered at the top of their lungs a couple hours earlier when I sang. Most people were happy to strike up a conversation and I was equally happy to spend time talking with them. The Blackhawks fans and I had developed a very special relationship. They had treated me with sincere and genuine appreciation for delivering their call to battle in the form of the Anthem, game after game for 13 memorable years.

As I left the Stadium that night, I left with only the memories. I would never sing there again. I do recall that night from the organ loft, high above the screaming crowd and the ice-covered plane of battle. Like so many times before, I sang the Anthem proudly and sincerely. I was accompanied by the mighty Barton Theater Organ that bellowed away as I accepted the challenge of trying to let my voice ring out over the leather-lunged encouragement of more than 16,000 fans who were worked up into a fever pitch.

The National Anthem at a Blackhawks game in venerable Chicago Stadium had evolved into an event unto itself. The fans would react with such enthusiasm that by the last eight measures of the song, my voice was barely audible over the almost maniacal outburst of screaming, clapping and cheering from the faithful throng of regulars.

It was an experience which could only be appreciated in person. Many had called it one of the most exciting moments in all of sports. I did not keep exact count, but I had probably sung more than 700 times for the boys with the Indian head crest on their sweaters. It was an experience that most people would relish to have had only once in their life. I said a prayer of thanks after each performance.

The memories were plentiful. From my perch in the organ loft, I had collected a series of unforgettable moments.

It was the famous site of the players lined up on the blue lines, an image of an event that has been captured perhaps more than any other moment in the rich and wonderful tradition of the Blackhawks. I used to wish that it would last forever.

What I could not possibly have realized earlier that night was that it had already ended. Thoughts of that night's Anthem – or the Blackhawks game – were not present in my mind as I walked south on Laughlin Street as I had done many times in the past after a post-game visit to Hawkeye's. I was focused on the upcoming weekend. I had left a voicemail message for Kathleen, asking her for a date on Saturday night. With our hectic schedules, we often found ourselves at two different events at the same time. That meant we had to schedule time together just to make sure that we could sit down and enjoy each other's company.

I would be on my way home within the hour. I would see my wife and I could enjoy some much-needed rest. It had been a very tiring week. I had worked some long hours at the office, where I had been working with my staff, crafting the business and marketing plans for the Chicago Wolves Hockey Team, which was scheduled to begin playing in the Fall. But I was especially excited about the fact that on the upcoming Sunday afternoon, the ABC Television Network was going to broadcast the Hawks versus the Los Angeles Kings game on national TV. The word was out that the National Anthem was going to be shown. And, to make things even better, describing the action would be Al Michaels, the announcer of the famed, "Do You Believe in Miracles," call from the USA Hockey Team's win in the 1980 Winter Olympics in Lake Placid, NY.

Being able to watch the Blackhawks play a home game on TV was about as rare as change from a street newspaper vendor. This would really be a big deal. I was excited about the national exposure. ABC had caught some heat locally and nationally when a televised game at the stadium a few weeks earlier had been in a commercial break while the place was customarily up for grabs during the Anthem. They put the word out to the fans almost as a challenge. If they were going to televise the Anthem, the fans had better be part of the show as well. Hawks' fans are not a group to toy with. They were ready, and they welcomed the rest of the country to watch how it was done in Chicago.

These were my thoughts at about 1:35 a.m. as I walked out the front door of Hawkeye's and stepped directly into my nightmare. I had taken the same path over a dozen times before without incident. I noticed how the area was well lit around the playground at Thomas Jefferson School. I couldn't help but think of the kids who laughed, played and skinned their knees on the same turf I was now walking on. This was their neighborhood schoolyard, a place of safety and innocent youth – or so I thought.

As I crossed the street approaching my car, I spotted a tall young man walking toward me. He was about four car lengths down the street to the east of where I was parked. The sight of him startled me. I quickly unlocked the driver's side door, entered the car and immediately started the engine. As I did this, the peaceful silence of the evening was interrupted by two loud noises, which I was to learn much later, were the sound of the cold metal of the handgun banging on the window of the car door, which I had shut behind me just a few seconds earlier.

Accompanying these piercing sounds were the shouts of the 15-year-old, who was flashing his prized possession, a 9mm pistol. I didn't hear his words. They were drowned out by the noise of him banging the gun on the glass of the driver's side window, just inches from my head. I didn't respond to him, since I was unaware that he was even there and had run up on me. I flinched from the two loud noises that I mistakenly thought were gunshots, which prompted me to get to safety. Almost by instinct, I put the car into reverse and made a fast move to pull the car away from the curb. It was then that I heard the third noise. This was the sound of the young criminal pulling the trigger of the gun, pointed directly at my head.

It was fired at point-blank range, from a distance he later described in court as, "so close, his elbow was touching the glass." The blow shattered the window, covering both of us with shards of glass.

Realizing what he had just done, the gunman stepped back to avoid getting hit by the car as I jammed my foot down on the gas pedal. Left empty-handed in the foiled robbery attempt, he took off running. The 16-year-old, at this moment little more than an eye-witness to the crime, was frozen in his tracks. He stood in disbelief at what had just happened right in front of him. In his moment of fear, his expression became the indelible image I would carry with me as my only vivid memory of the incident.

As I sped passed this young man, I saw him as possibly the only eye witness to what could be my murder-in-progress. His face was etched permanently into my memory, a vivid image that I would be called upon to identify in the courtroom.

Things had not gone as planned. The fool-proof scheme had turned against them. There was nothing to show for their efforts. My wallet and $52 in cash were still in my pocket. They had not stolen my car. They had, in fact, accomplished only one thing. Both young men – the 15-year-old who pulled the trigger and the 16-year-old who would equally share the guilt by his mere presence on the scene – had just branded themselves as criminals. As they ran off to their nearby homes to escape the police, I recognized that my journey was just beginning.

Charged with fear and adrenaline, I drove the car around the corner and across Taylor Street, virtually retracing the path that I had just walked. Pulling to the curb next to Hawkeyes, I quickly got out, made my way to the front door and up the steps where people were still laughing and talking. My entrance brought a chill to the celebration almost instantly. The moment I came through the front door, it was apparent that something very bad had happened.

Almost in shock from fear already, I became even more frightened when I attempted to speak. Instead of the baritone voice that had taken me to a career as a broadcaster, singer and speaker for nearly 20 years, there was only a marginally audible sound. Much like a gurgling death rattle where a voice used to be.

I could only mouth the words, "I've been shot." Someone opened the door, which had been locked, as was the policy later in the evening. As the crowd realized what happened, someone quickly called 911 to dispatch an ambulance and a police car. I sat down on a bench near the front door, fully aware of the seriousness of the situation. I recognized that I had just been shot at close range in the throat. I wasn't sure whether or not I had already been dealt the final hand. I was scared and upset. "Shot in the throat!" I screamed inside of myself, unable to make a sound. "Now what?"

As I waited for the Chicago Fire Department Ambulance to arrive, I told myself that dying was not an option. As my blood soaked my white shirt, I fought to maintain my composure. It was obvious that the injuries were serious. It was also obvious that I may be facing some serious changes and challenges in my life as a result of this experience. But all that would come later. Right now, I was concerned with doing what I needed to just live long enough to get to the hospital. I prayed for help. I had to have faith that the E.R. surgeons on duty were the right men and women for the job. I prayed that God was watching over me in this time of desperate need and I prayed that my guardian angel had not taken the day off.

I still had no idea where the bullet had come from or who had pulled the trigger. All I knew was that I had seen someone who had witnessed the shooting and I knew that I could identify that face. Despite having this invaluable bit of information, I was suddenly and uncomfortably trapped in my own silence with a bullet dangerously lodged in my neck.

The Save the Children Foundation© tie that I was wearing was covered with the illustrated faces of smiling children and flags from around the world. It was still firmly affixed around the collar of my blood-stained shirt. The tie had lodged itself into the entry wound and prevented the massive blood loss that usually accompanies a gunshot wound to the neck.

In an incredibly ironic twist, this festive tie was designed by another 15-year-old boy to raise money to help other children and it had actually served to save my life from a gunshot wound inflicted by another 15-year-old.

Although the bleeding was lessened, it was still substantial. I sat quietly, almost motionless while nervously waiting out the approximately 10 minutes for the paramedics to arrive. The usually boisterous crowd was silenced by the drama they were witnessing. A couple of the Blackhawks players were still there. I remember looking at Dirk Graham, making eye contact with the team captain, who looked at me in disbelief. Everyone, including me, felt completely helpless.

As I sat there in shock, Kristine – a young hockey fan and a friend, but more significantly a nursing student – came to my immediate assistance. She stepped forward when everyone else stood frozen in their own spot, keeping just enough distance to watch what was happening, but not getting involved. Her first aid intervention and comforting words during these critical moments helped to significantly ease my fear as we all held our breath for the arrival of the ambulance. I was enormously grateful for her help.

Medical assistance came shortly after two uniformed police officers came on the scene. I was unable to speak, yet I was able to motion that my car was just outside and that I had been shot. Of course, this was fairly obvious to the police and to the paramedics.

As I was transported onto the gurney and into the mobile intensive care unit, I kept motioning that they needed to call my wife. I pointed to my wedding ring and held my hand up to my ear like I was holding a telephone. I made it clear that I did not want to go into surgery without Kathleen knowing where I was and why I was there. My fear started to mount. I did not want to die. Certainly not without seeing Kathleen's face one more time. I gained courage and strength by keeping her image in my heart and in my mind. I told myself over and over again, "No matter what happens, dying is not an option here."

As we arrived at Cook County Hospital, I was fighting to stay in control of my emotions and my life. Despite all that had happened, I remained lucid, yet I could feel myself starting to slip out of consciousness. It was becoming increasingly more difficult to breath. The swelling in my throat was starting to close up the air passage and the blood was starting to well up in my throat, along with the tears in my eyes. It had now been approximately 45 minutes since I had been shot. I was still awake, waiting, hoping and praying when I gave into unconsciousness. I would remain that way until Tuesday afternoon, two and a half days later. As I drifted off, I did not know if I would wake up again. I had not been able to see Kathleen's face in person, but she was there with me in my heart.

The following day after I had regained consciousness, I lay in recovery, the first arrest was made. The shooter had been picked up and questioned by police. Then he confessed. He had implicated the person I had spotted on the crime scene. All of this had transpired without any assistance from me.

Now, as I stood in the courtroom three years later, the flashback images of the entire episode were as real as the moment they happened. The awakening moment came as the judge sounded out his ruling of the sentence. I watched the face of the accused, looking for some indication that he was as evil as the prosecutors had portrayed him. I wanted to hate. I wanted to lash out, but I couldn't.

It had been three years, two months and twenty-two days since I had walked into a nightmare. It seemed like yesterday, yet it seemed like a lifetime ago. In many ways, it was. The time had reeled in my mind in just a few seconds. As I waited for the judge to put this lingering episode to rest, I knew right then why I had fought so hard to stay alive. It was all suddenly so crystal clear. I knew that it was all a bonus. Every minute of every day, I was in overtime. I knew it.

Once again, I clutched the hand of my wife. I gazed into her tear-filled eyes and those of my mother and sister who had joined us for this moment. As I did, I warmly enjoyed the memory of the weekend that had just passed, as Kathleen and I watched our beautiful daughter, Jennifer, walk down the aisle. This was a vision that I would always treasure in my heart, as what I remember with great emotion the song my wife and I were able to sing together for our lovely bride. I also felt the love we shared as we held each other's hands, remembering the music we now were once again able to share, having to make it up the steep and often difficult road to recovery. It was all worth the fight. We had made it back from the depths of despair and disappointment. Our faith and our belief in each other had pulled us through.

"Why aren't we celebrating at this moment?" I asked myself. There were no shouts of joy knowing that this person who stood before the judge was being sent to prison. He would later be sentenced to concurrent terms of eight years for attempted aggravated battery, 12 years for attempted armed robbery and 21 years for attempted first degree murder. There was no cause to celebrate the destruction of a young man's life because he was at the scene of the crime. I felt sickened that they were, as I put it, "hanging the wrong guy."

It was a sad and painful experience to watch the proceedings. Was there closure? That was the question everyone asked me. I'm afraid the answer was positively no, there was not. Along with the sadness of the moment, there was also joy. The joy came in knowing that I had indeed survived to tell the story.

As I walked out of the courtroom and felt the summer sun on our faces, I looked at Kathleen and spoke in my full, rich baritone voice, words coming from the bottom of my heart. "It's a great day to be alive," I said. Through her comforting smile, she replied, "It sure is."

26

Prosecutors try to charge suspect in Messmer shooting as an adult

--The Chicago Tribune

"Courage is the price that life exacts for granting peace."
--Amelia Earhart

Messmer Kin awaits word on his Voice
--The Chicago Sun-Times

"We are not interested in the possibilities of defeat."
--Queen Victoria

Chapter 3:
The "Real E.R."

Saturday through Tuesday,
April 9 through 12, 1994

Trauma Unit, Cook County Hospital - Chicago

I remained amazingly alert throughout the transport via the ambulance to Cook County Hospital. Yet, I was frightened by the passing of time. Each second, I feared may have been bringing me closer to my last breath. As the anxiety level increased, so too did the difficulty in hanging on to consciousness. Finally, I gave into the moment and slipped away from the gripping reality of what was happening to me. As I did, the nightmare was just about to place its ugly hands on my family.

The ringing phone in the bedroom of our home startled Kathleen. It was never a good sign to get a call that late at night. By the time the hospital called her, it was already past 2:00a.m. The words she would hear would start her heart racing in fear. After identifying himself as Dr. Seth Krosner from Cook County Hospital, the surgeon broke the news that I had been shot in the neck. "Shot?!" Kathleen shouted back in the phone. "He's a singer. His voice is important to him." "We know who he is and what he does," Dr. Krosner responded with a comforting tone. "How soon can you get here?" he sternly asked.

Moments like this are infrequent in our lives. But when they do happen, we discover our own ability to react to them. Some respond better than others, but we have no choice other than to spring into action. Not surprisingly,

Kathleen did just that. Her first reaction was to realize she needed some help to make sure that she could safely get to the hospital. Driving alone, she thought, would not be a good idea. Picking up the phone with trembling hands, she dialed the number of our closest neighbors and dear friends, whose front door was about 50 feet from our back door. Just as she had been abruptly interrupted from her sleep by the phone, the same scene was now playing out next door.

Tom and Sherry were friends who were usually surrounded with laughter and music in our frequent times together. This was altogether different. As Tom heard the news from Kathleen, he dropped the phone on the kitchen floor and stood motionless in shock. After a matter of a few seconds, the plan was activated. They would drive together to Cook County Hospital and see firsthand exactly how bad the situation was and what there was to be done.

Before they could leave, Kathleen had to make a second call. This one to my parents. Delivering the news in the middle of the night to the two people who could not have been prouder of all of my accomplishments had to be devastatingly painful. Their son, whose voice had given them so much enjoyment over the years, was now silenced. The questions immediately poured out. Yet, there were no answers to be given. No one knew what to ask, afraid of what the response might be. The only thing they could all agree on in the brief moments of their emotional exchange was that they all needed to get to the hospital as soon as possible.

Within the hour, they all converged in a cluttered waiting room at the trauma unit to support each other as they waited throughout the night to hear the next update on my status. Everyone arrived before I was taken into surgery. The ER was filled with victims. Some who had been shot in confrontations with the police were handcuffed to their beds.

Others who were wounded by gang violence from the surrounding streets were clinging to life. Some of those would lose this fight.

After what must have seemed like an endless period of time, the scene was intensified as Kathleen was shown an x-ray of the vital areas of my neck. A female doctor pointed out the close proximity of the bullet to the main artery to my heart, as well as to my spine. As my wife looked at the image, the horror of the situation hit her. There I was, motionless and within her vision, perhaps unable to sing or talk again. We could not have known at that point in time. But yet, alive. I could have easily been paralyzed or, worse yet, killed instantly had the bullet taken a path just a few centimeters either way.

Kathleen was given a glimpse as to what lay ahead in the next several weeks as early Saturday morning arrived. She was handed a note with some names on it for her to call. These were concerned people who had already heard the news of the shooting on the radio and TV, where it was a headline story. She realized she'd better make some more calls to let the rest of the family know what was happening before they heard it on a newscast.

Almost immediately, a TV reporter accompanied by his cameramen were standing face to face with my wife, who was thrust into the center of a whirlwind of confusion. At this point, I was still in surgery. If there was any news at all, even my family didn't know it yet.

Early that morning, my friend and business associate, Grant Mulvey, arrived at the hospital and immediately assumed the role of disaster coordinator, stepping forward to handle the media. He was the person who had recruited me to help on the project of building the new Chicago Wolves Professional Hockey Team. His background as a professional athlete, coupled with his outgoing personality, prepared him for the moment. His intervention was even more appreciated since he gave my family a sense of comfort and protection as they continued to wait out the minutes that had now turned into hours.

Grant assumed the role of spokesperson and announced that there would be a press conference on the hospital grounds that afternoon to try and communicate the details of the situation. Details which were still hours away. After what seemed to be an interminable wait, Dr. Krosner entered the waiting room. The almost 10 hours of surgery was finally over. The bullet was out. Krosner said he was fairly positive and pleased with the outcome. The vital areas had not been damaged, the bullet had not passed through the vocal cords, but it may have damaged the voice box.

His explanation was simultaneously comforting and confusing since there were so many hypothetical questions that could not be answered at that time. Kathleen and my mother were the first to see me after emerging from the operating room. Their trip to my bed in the trauma unit brought fear with each step. Their fears were realized when they came upon me. I had been attached to a ventilator, had undergone a tracheotomy, leaving a large plastic tube emerging from my throat and I was I being hydrated by multiple IVs.

Additionally, there was a large tube down my nose and a drain tube coming out of each side of my neck, which had swollen to a circumference wider than my head. It must have been quite a sight.

Before anyone knew it, the time had flown by and the 2:00 p.m. press conference was underway. The whole city of Chicago and the wire services were now aware of the tragedy. I have no idea where these days went or where I traveled with them. There was an advantage, I suppose, to having slipped away from the scene at Cook County Hospital where my poor wife had been holding up like a giant.

The conversation I would have expected to have – namely, the great mortality debate – was actually lost somewhere in a morphine-induced haze on the west side of Chicago. I was also being spared the nightmare of discovering that moving my fingers and toes would have to wait. Doctors had placed me in a medically-induced state of temporary paralysis for my own safety. The trouble was that upon awakening, I had no way of knowing the temporary nature of the condition.

The issues of what could have been had already been addressed by Kathleen, who had that discussion with the surgical trauma team at CCH. It was so early, I didn't even know for sure where I was or what had transpired. Although, the facts concerning the reason I was there at all were very clear – even to me, under heavy sedation. In my hallucinating semi-conscious state, my unfamiliar surroundings reminded me of something from a time long ago. I saw images of serpents, gargoyles and reptiles affixed to the wall. It all seemed to fit in with the rest of the décor – gang members and an abounding sense of violence and its consequences.

There seemed to be a couple staff members with whom I felt I could communicate in this M.A.S.H.-like environment. I found out much later that several friends had come by to "view the body." I recall only a few vague images of faces as I passed through various stages of consciousness. None of them was recognizable. The sights and smells of the intensive care unit were foreign to me.

As I gazed around the trauma unit at Cook County Hospital, I wondered just how bad things were. My instincts weren't responding. I wanted to call out for answers to my growing list of questions. I wondered silently what was happening as the medical staff moved by the bedside at a frightening pace, only stopping long enough to cast a quick glance in my direction. I was searching for a clue in their expressions as to the severity of my condition. It was apparent that no one was talking, especially me.

The feeling of helplessness was augmented by the sense of immobility that had grasped by entire being. Every ounce of energy had been taken from me. I wanted to cry. I wanted to cry out loud. Neither of which I was able to do. Exactly what was going on? I knew that I had been shot in the throat and the prognosis could be anything ranging from a life in total silence to a full and complete recovery or any one of hundreds of steps along the way. I wanted to know, but I feared the news that would be slow in coming.

Immediately, I began to have a discussion with myself to lessen the anxiety welling up inside of me. There were no textbook responses to the fears, no form letters to be read. Mine was a delicate situation in as much as the doctors and nurses were concerned and, as a result, everyone was reluctant to speak to me without being able to tell me what everyone was asking. Will he ever sing again?

To be honest, that was not the most important thing on my mind. I was concerned about being alive and staying that way. Although, the persistent questions about my voice did linger deep inside of me. Hoping for a clue, I tried to clear my voice and discovered a painful and uneasy sensation like nothing I had ever felt before. It was apparent that the damage was substantial. The likelihood of resuming the career I had crafted over the past several years was now in jeopardy of coming to an abrupt halt. While unable to move, I was spending the conscious time trying to catch a glimpse of reality. Several times, I felt I had been overtaken with an overwhelming feeling of oppression. I felt helpless.

The shooting had already altered my life. I was more afraid of the waking moments than anything else at that point. As I felt myself slipping into and out of consciousness, I searched for something to hold on to. That anchor of hope came in two forms: my wife and a belief that God would watch over me in this time of need.

I had been shielded from the media coverage surrounding the shooting incident. It was fortunate since just trying to cope with the trauma and the severity of the injury was enough pressure. It was about at this point in the experience where I finally submitted to unconsciousness, a state I remained in for two-and-a-half days.

Upon waking, I realized that the dream was real. My new home was Cook County Hospital's Intensive Care Unit on the city's West Side. This facility actually carries a worldwide reputation for expertise in trauma and emergency care, but the physical appearance of the place did leave a lot to be desired. The Chicago Fire Department ambulance paramedic crew of Henry and Bill who had transported me there knew the reputation and took me where I'd receive the best attention... and this place was it.

Waking up to an unknown situation is frightening enough. But when forced to make the assessment of the quality of life you've been left with, after fighting so hard to stay alive, it becomes an even heavier load to bear. It was too early to tell what kind of voice, if any, I would ever have again. I realized I was not as concerned about the National Anthem spotlight or returning to the radio studio as much as I was concerned about the fact that I might never have the opportunity again to sing with my wife. This thought was ever present as Kathleen kept a bedside vigil, with an inner strength that was truly a moving force for me and the rest of the family.

What do I ask? What do they know? What aren't they telling me that my family already knows? Why aren't they telling me something? Anything? These were just a few of the countless questions that were circling my mind like a recurring nightmare. Unable to verbalize my thoughts and communicate in an intelligent train of thought, I felt isolated, stranded and very much alone.

The actual events of the incident were not as terrifying as not knowing the extent of the injuries I had suffered. I was there physically and, to a lesser degree, mentally. But I felt invisible. Both my personality and my spirit were searching for a resting place. I knew that my soul and my will to live were present with me in that hospital bed. That alone was enough to keep me on a course of sanity. Looking around, I discovered the breathing apparatus, the multiple bags of intravenous solution feeding vital fluids back in to my starved body. I knew that I was hooked up to machines which were helping me in my battle to stay alive. But just how long were these tubes and heavy machinery be a part of me?

Depending on a respirator to breathe was a frustrating and uncomfortable feeling. Especially when coupled with everything else that was going on. I had never spent the night in a hospital before this. In fact, I had never had a stitch. This innocence left me unprepared for how to act as a patient. There is quite definitely a patient protocol, but I was unaware.

I was unaware of plenty of other things, too. I felt awkward and uneasy spending time in a foreign bed. It was something I knew I would not warm up to. I didn't like it at all one bit. More than anything, I just wanted to talk to Kathleen and ask her to help me. I needed to be told that it would be all right, that I was going to live. I needed to hear that no matter what else may happen, we'd figure it out together. I was content just being alive, but increasingly more fearful of what might happen next.

It was as if I had dropped a priceless statue and I was delaying the moment of truth where I would look to see how badly it had been damaged. I wondered if they would be able to put the pieces back together, whether my voice would suffer the fate of Humpty Dumpty, who never did quite get it together again. The priceless statue was my voice and the pieces were the insecurity of what might possibly be ahead, not just today, but in the months and years to follow.

The insistent sound of beeping monitors and the rhythmic pulsation of the respirator was scaring me to the point where I was starting to anticipate that the truth was about to be known. I tried to convince myself that if I just rested quietly, everything would be fine. Although, deep down, I knew better.

I found the fact that I was a first-time hospital patient fairly remarkable as I reflected over the close calls from high school and college. I was used to being a healthy person, but now my life was totally in the hands of other people. The loss of independence became more noticeable by the minute. The very fact that I was depending on these machines to keep me alive was the most disturbing element of my entrapment.

Trying to provide a distraction from the incessant sounds of the ICU, Kathleen brought me a cassette player and a couple tapes. She had selected Frank Sinatra and Rodney Dangerfield as the headliners to help me escape from the moment. They really helped.

I could not help but wonder how long it had been since I was first brought into the E.R. My sense of time had long been distorted beyond the point where I could regain perspective. I worried about how long the respirator and the other life supports would remain attached. I was afraid to move, fearing I might not be able to. I was concerned that my family was experiencing more pain than I was. It seemed rather curious to me that my pain level was actually quite low. Was it the medication, I wondered? Or, had I been hurt badly enough so that pain would no longer be a part of my life? Separating fact from fiction became a full-time job. Deciding between truth and hallucination was almost impossible. I saw faces, some more recognizable and others were faint and distant. The only constant was the overwhelming sensation of helplessness.

Here it was, Spring in my hometown. My favorite season of the year. When nature would once again blossom into something. But to me, that was lightyears away. Outside the walls of the Cook County Hospital, where I lay incarcerated by a bullet wound, held hostage by my own injury.

There were several of us in the trauma ward. Strangers who were all sharing the same misfortune of having crossed the path that brought us to this dreary place. The ward was filled with sadness, but I got the feeling it was also filled with immeasurable hope. As I counted the moments as best I could, I started to see the sense of trust beginning to take root. I knew that I had to trust the fact that the surgeons were careful to have done their craft with regard to my vocal instrument. But even at that point, I knew without doubt that it had been bent, but not broken.

There were flashbacks of the moment of arrival at County when the paramedics delivered me into the hands of the ER surgeons in a state of shock and confusion. I recall the minutes leading up to the surgery. My memory took me to the point where the swelling in my throat, coupled with the internal bleeding, had forced the need for the radical tracheotomy. I remember being sedated before they opened my throat. I vividly recall the helpless feeling of gasping for breath and beginning to panic when I lost consciousness.

The memories were as surreal as the distorted views that cluttered my vision. The police officers, the paramedics, the doctors and nurses were all characters I had seen on TV and in movies. My life experience as a child of the TV Generation was actually helping me to rationalize the moment by desensitizing my fear. I hoped for a happy ending for the episode in which I was involved. I kept telling myself that things would work out, although I was still very uncertain of the complexities of the plot, which had not yet been revealed.

Coupled with the distorted perspective was the fact that I was unable to see very well without my glasses. This was a problem I was going to have to deal with since I was unable to ask for them or even motion that I wanted them. Remember, the surgeons had placed me in a state of temporary paralysis until they were able to assess the injury more clearly. This condition was also something that I remained unaware of. This did not help to answer any burning questions about the effect of the shooting on my neuromuscular system.

I was unable to ignore the fact that no one was speaking directly to me. People were standing over me and some were speaking, but I could not make sense of it and I was certainly unable to respond in any manner. More and more, I was sensing a feeling of desperation with an enormous level of frustration, all combining to create an almost consuming sense of melancholy, which I feared might swallow me alive.

Wayne Messmer

On April 11, 1994

Jay Mariotti wrote The Chicago Sun-Times'

Without Messmer, Stadium Is Cold And Empty Place

They didn't try to outshout the Anthem Sunday. Instead, 18,000 hockey maniacs were unusually subdued, realizing the tender importance of letting Wayne Messmer's voice boom through the stadium. Usually, noise is the best tribute to the man. On this day, it was restraint at the start followed by a loud burst for tradition's sake.

For one afternoon in April Memorex sufficed. Fans hung homemade signs: "Hurry back, Wayne," "Get well, Wayne," "It's just not the same without Wayne," and dab their eyes when, as always, he stretched the final resounding "brave" over two syllables. But from here on, mere recordings of Messmer's powerful baritone just aren't going to work. Not now. Not with the Old Barn closing down. Tapes will just make us angry; they will remind us how wretched the world can be, how unfair it has been to a gentleman who never did anything wrong but give his hometown a lot of goosebumps.

He apparently is going to recover from a bullet wound in the neck, thank heavens. "He wiggled his toes and then squeezed my hand," said ex-Blackhawk, Grant Mulvey, Messmer's close friend and business partner. "Wayne's going to make it." Still, the story is horribly tragic. It's possible Wayne Messmer, having been shot precisely close to his vocal cords in what police say was a failed robbery attempt, never will sing again. Worse yet, it's unlikely he'll be able to close down the stadium with his nightly rendition, which is like closing down the neighborhood bar without Sinatra. They should add it to the list of criminal charges.

Keeping Messmer away from the building in its final days is the biggest sin of all. Such trauma isn't what The Barn had in mind for its swan song. First, Bill Wirtz goes pyrotechnic on us and says he wants to blow up the place, explode decades of memories with tender loving

40

dynamite. Now the singer who gave The Stadium its energy in old age rests at Cook County Hospital, recovering from 10 hours of surgery that saved his life. What's next? The Barton organ falling from the loft? The fog horn turning into a kazoo?

Rarely does anyone regard an Anthem singer with gushy fondness, but Messmer has been that special to us, an institution in a sports town that doesn't award the distinction liberally. You can go to stadiums and arenas around the America, the world over, and never see a scene like the Messmer Anthem. News accounts are listing him from his work with the Cubs and his executive position with the new International Hockey League franchise, along with past duties for the White Sox and Sting. But hockey nights at The Stadium always will be his niche, the act that made him famous. I tell people in other towns, "I'm from Chicago," and they sometimes say, "I'll never forget that singer who gave everyone the chills during the Persian Gulf War." The moment at the 1991 NHL All-Star Game not only made him a treasure, but showed how sports can bring hope to a troubled world and produced the most tingling patriotic salutes.

As much as anyone, including a dream-maker named Jordan, Messmer gave The Stadium a renaissance of sorts in the '80s. Before then, it was known as an aging sports temple – filled, but not always dramatic for Hawks' games, rarely filled and often lifeless for Bulls games. Messmer helped make the building magical with the aid of some leather- lunged fans on a May evening in 1985. At least a million of you were there, I know.

Down two games to none to Wayne Gretzky and Edmonton, the crowd tried to arouse the Hawks in the conference final by shouting over The Star Spangled Banner. That took some doing, because the voice of Messmer, before then known as The Dude Who Sings the Anthem, was almighty. But they managed to drown him out, which lead to a Hawks victory. They lost the series, but a chilling Chicago tradition was born.

Wayne Messmer

The Hawks won another game on Sunday, surviving the Gretzky Los Angeles Kings for a two to one victory. But the effort was surprisingly uninspired, given the obvious drama.

If any luck can be found in an awful story, it's that the bullet didn't strike Messmer's vocal cords. Remarkably, it missed by millimeters. At this time, doctors won't offer a prognosis about whether he'll sing again. They're happy he's alive. Shot allegedly by a 15-year-old near Hawkeye's Bar and Grill, a post-game haunt on Taylor Street. The fantasy, of course, is to see the Hawks shock their way into the Stanley Cup Finals. Then, from the Zamboni gate, Wayne Messmer walks onto the ice and belts out the Anthem before Game One. No man more deserves a miracle.

Cubs React With Anger To Messmer Shooting

--The Chicago Sun-Times

"He that cannot forgive others breaks the bridge over which he must pass himself."
--Thomas Fuller

Wayne Messmer

No Wayne: 'It's Just Not The Same...'
--The Chicago Tribune

"Wayne Messmer's Anthem at Chicago Stadium - one of the most exciting moments in sports"
--Al Michaels

Chapter 4

Sorry, I Won't Be Attending the Party

Wednesday, April 13, 1994

The Arrival at Northwestern Memorial Hospital

After four days, I was taken out of Cook County Hospital. The surgeons had worked their magic to keep me alive, despite the trying conditions for all of us involved. On the first day there, I discovered that I had been placed in the VIP section of the hospital, where I was registered under the name of Ralph Kramden, Jackie Gleason's famed alter ego character from the 1950s television series, *The Honeymooners,* although the nurses spelled Kramden with a C instead of a K. When Kathleen was asked to provide an alias to divert the press corps on the deluge of attention from the curious public, she did not pause a second without knowing that my hero, "Old Ralphie Boy," would be my first choice too.

The time had come to put my trust into a new set of healing hands. This was all so foreign to me. I felt as though I had little or no control over the situation or of my recovery. From what I could tell, the facilities were nice, the staff seemed concerned and my sweet wife was going to stay with me on my first night in the new surroundings. They brought in a rollaway bed for her. She had been through so much already, I just hoped that she would be able to handle it okay.

I couldn't help but think about how there were a lot of places I'd rather be than where I was. Even with the VIP

45

treatment and the private room, this was a frightening experience. I was uncomfortable in my situation and even more uncomfortable in knowing the fact that I was mute.

Thursday, April 14, 1994

This was the day that was supposed to be the big one at Chicago Stadium for me. It was the final regular season game in the history of the grand old building that had proudly sat on West Madison Street through its glory days in 1924 until this night. Next season, the Blackhawks and the Bulls would move to a new home across the street. It would be new and fresh and shiny. Oh, it would have all the trimmings of the finest arenas around, but the building it was replacing carried with it memories of several generations of Chicagoans, including many of my fondest moments in sports.

It was there that I first saw and heard the voice of Frank Sinatra, where I began my singing and announcing career with the Chicago Sting Soccer Team and where my longtime love affair with Blackhawks' fans had been spawned and nurtured over the years. This was the last scheduled regular season home game before the playoffs. It was to be special. It was not to be missed.

When I first got my tickets at the beginning of the season, I knew I had to share this one with my sweetheart. Little did I know how the scene would play out.

Medically, I was in better shape, relatively speaking - thanks to a downsizing of the tracheostomy tube, but I was not really sure that I knew what that meant. Did it mean something less obtrusive or were they preparing me for a lifetime of breathing through a tube in my throat? All I could do was stand by and wait for the details to unmask themselves.

Kathleen told me that the Blackhawks had asked her to represent us at tonight's game. I knew this was going to be emotional. Communicating indirectly through Kathleen, I had made a request and was granted the chance to prepare a written statement to be read by their veteran play-by-play announcer, Pat Foley, on the air that night as part of the game's opening ceremonies. I recognized that I would have to give it some very serious thought.

I remember feeling cheated for the first time since the incident. I really wanted to be there tonight. In fact, I felt as though I had spent 13 years in preparation for the evening and it had been stolen from me. I scribbled down some thoughts on what to say and I found myself fumbling for words. "Thanks. Wish I were there. Sorry I'm not. Please be nice to my sweetheart." I probably needed a little more than that, I told myself.

But I knew that that theme of my message was captured in this simple statement I had just written down. Eventually, after some thought, I sketched out some ideas which seemed to flow naturally from my heart and seemed to almost write themselves. The message was read with great emotion to the stadium crowd and over the air. I listened on the radio I borrowed from the nurses' station. It was a moment to remember. When completed, it read as follows:

It is with deep disappointment that I am unable to be with you on this historic evening to celebrate what Chicago Stadium has meant to all of us for so many years. For 13 seasons, we have shared very personal moments together, from the NHL All-Star Game to the Stanley Cup Finals, to the final night when the roar of the regular season comes to an end.

As you have heard, five days ago, my voice was silenced by a senseless and careless act of random violence. I need your support and prayers in what will be the most difficult challenge of my life. To the boys on the ice, all of you fans and the Blackhawks organization, I thank you for cheering, your enthusiasm and your support. As for the stadium, I say, "Goodbye, old girl. I'll never forget you."

Sincerely,

Wayne

Foley then continued and turned the attention to my superhero who was there, standing in the exact spot in the organ loft where I had celebrated so many times before with the great fans as we lifted our voices in boisterous patriotism.

Ladies and gentlemen, we direct your attention to the organ loft. There's a woman named Kathleen Messmer up there. Kathleen, over the years, Wayne has provided thousands of Chicagoans a sense of national pride. He has instilled enthusiasm and energy in many, many Blackhawks fans. We are hoping tonight that, to the best of your ability, you can take the energy and the enthusiasm that you're going to feel right now and take it back to Wayne so he knows how badly we all want him to get better.

Ladies and gentlemen, Wayne Messmer is not here in person, but he is here on tape so we can hear his sterling rendition of the Canadian National Anthem. Then, ladies and gentlemen, make Wayne proud, do yourselves proud. Let's see if we can't raise the roof in this place during the Star-Spangled Banner.

The Canadian National Anthem with me singing was then played.

Now, here is Wayne's rendition of The Star Spangled Banner.

When *The Star Spangled Banner* began with the introduction, the Stadium erupted in cheers, whistles and a level of enthusiasm that had to be experienced in person to fully appreciate

Ladies and gentlemen, that's Chicago Stadium. That's hockey.

My mom and dad were at my bedside as we huddled near the radio, listening to what was happening. It was a genuine outpouring of love from the Blackhawks fans and from the City of Chicago.

I was starting to get a sense of the scope of the magnitude of my personal crisis. I continued to search for a reason for why this ever happened at all. My wife was the star of the show. She would shine throughout the entire experience with a sense of immense dedication and strength. I knew that I was truly blessed to have been paired in my life with such an amazing partner.

Following the broadcast, I was taken downstairs for a CT scan on my throat and neck. The procedure brought my emotions down very quickly. With the sudden crash from the state of euphoria produced by the events of the night, I felt a tremendous loneliness as I was inserted into the tube for the procedure. The sentimental moment of joy suddenly gave way to a painfully melancholy dark cloud hanging over my scared and wounded head.

The reality of what had been stolen from me with this crime was never more stunningly apparent. I gasped for breath, unable to hold back the flow of tears. It was obvious to me that I had hit the bottom. The only way to go now was up. But I could sense the enormous difficulties of the path that lay ahead of me.

Wayne Messmer

On April 11, 1994
Mike Imrem wrote in The Daily Herald

Sad Day indeed For Soon-To Be-Gone Stadium

The Great One was a notable scratch from Sunday's Blackhawks' game in Chicago Stadium. Oh yeah, Wayne Gretzky didn't perform either. The Los Angeles Kings' Center, the number one scorer in hockey history, sprained his knee the day before in Winnipeg and might be out for the season.

As if Sunday's 18,472 ticket holders at The Stadium weren't already disappointed enough, they arrived on West Madison Street, aware that another Wayne – and in this case, not merely the "other Wayne," wouldn't be joining them. Wayne Messmer remained in Cook County Hospital after enduring a gunshot wound to the neck early Saturday morning and 10 hours of surgery later that day. No Gretzky, no Messmer. No wonder the Hawks' 2-1 victory was so blah.

Gretzky's injury, not nearly as serious or significant, was to a part of the anatomy that helped make him the best hockey player of all time. Messmer's was to the larynx that made him the Chicago's most inspirational singer of The Star Spangled Banner of all time. Messmer's condition was listed as stable, but serious Sunday. His situation, no longer considered life-threatening, did remain career threatening.

ABC's Al Michaels explained to a regional TV audience Sunday what The Stadium crowd already knew; the National Anthem would be tinged with sadness today because of Messmer's absence. This isn't the way it's supposed to be in this arena at this time, is it?

These are supposed to be glorious times for this stadium, winding down its final season before being replaced for hockey, basketball and other events by The United Center across the street. Gretzky was supposed to take one more majestic skate around the old building, rather than sitting down in the Kings' locker room, having his knee iced. The Stadium was supposed to be electric during these final regular season

50

Blackhawks' games Sunday against LA and Thursday night against Toronto.

Wayne Messmer's booming baritone voice was supposed to trigger it all by stoking the crowd through the Anthem. When they talk about remembering the roar, Messmer's voice is among the first things that come to mind. Instead, he was in a hospital bed Sunday afternoon, drifting in and out of consciousness in stable, but serious condition. Gone from The Stadium, but clearly not forgotten. Banners dangled from The Stadium's second balcony, reading "The Anthem won't be the same." "We wish you well, Wayne." "Hurry back, Wayne."

Messmer, shot on the West Side after a late meal following a Hawks' victory, was just one more Friday night/Saturday morning statistic. There were six murdered and 13 wounded in Chicago during this period. Almost routine numbers by today's standards. Hockey is supposed to be a cruel, violent game but it's pretty civil compared to man's inhumanity toward man out in the real world. Certainly, all shooting victims are special to their friends, to their families, to someone. The Messmer difference is he's special to an entire metropolitan area for his National Anthem, being PA Announcer at Wrigley Field and overall gracing the local sports scene.

To those who know him, he's a guy who always is pleasant, helpful and respectful. You'd have to go a ways to find somebody who would say anything bad about Wayne Messmer.

To those who never met him, he symbolizes something uniquely upbeat. I mean, what's more positive than a goosebumpy version of The Star Spangled Banner.

The frightening aspect of his predicament is that if this could happen to him, if somebody could do something like this to somebody like him, the message again is that nobody is immune anymore.

Sunday, Blackhawks' management decided to use a recorded version of Messmer singing the Anthem. Thursday may be a repeat or Wayne's wife, Kathleen, might be asked to substitute. Either would be

51

okay, but Chicago sports needs Wayne Messmer back as soon as possible. And, oh yeah, it would be nice if the other Great Wayne gets back on the ice for the Kings too.

Friday, April 15, 1994

Another long night of violent coughing kept me awake most of the evening. I had been told that it's a good thing to cough, so I kept grunting. I started the morning by picking up a newspaper and seeing a photo on the front page of the sports section in *The Chicago Tribune*. There, in full color, was a sign from the Blackhawks' game last night which read, "God bless Wayne Messmer." Thinking the person would take the time to make that banner and hold it proudly over their head for all to see overwhelmed me with emotion.

I was still having a hard time grasping just how immense the coverage of this event actually was. Kathleen described the one sign that captured the attention of the crowd above all others. It was a hand-painted sign on a bedsheet with a message of despair and frustration.

It read:

A fifteen-year-old with a handgun stole our Anthem

As I looked deeply into the faces in the picture holding the sign, it spoke to me of great memories of moments of passion that I had shared in the wonderful building, affectionately known as the "Old Barn." I was fully aware that it was an incredible privilege to have had the opportunity to sing there just once during a lifetime, yet I was given the chance to fill the room with music hundreds of times for 13 wonderful and magical years.

Memories of Chicago Stadium filled my mind. It was a priceless collection. Memories of laughter and cheers, shouts of triumph and sighs in times of defeat. In my time in this historic sports shrine, I was able to see and experience a great deal of all these emotions. For me, it was a very special place. It was there that I first sang for a professional sporting event, with Chicago's championship soccer team, the Chicago Sting, back in 1980.

It was also the place that grew to become home for a very special moment in time, captured over and over again before each Blackhawks game. It was not me as much as it was the fans who were always the show during the tradition. I was proud to be the singer of the National Anthem at Chicago Stadium. The anticipation at the start of the game and the spontaneous emotions swelling throughout the building were brought about by the ever-present crowd of more than 16,000 Chicagoans who were always up for the challenge of rocking the house, night after night. We had worked in harmony over the years to create a special moment of deafening madness that captured a lethal dose of patriotism with anticipation for the ensuing battle on the ice.

I had always recognized how fortunate I had been to be the guy who was singing while the revolution was in progress. The moment was to be immortalized in a marketing campaign introduced in the last season in the building. It called on fans to remember the roar. The fact is, anyone who had ever experienced it, could not possibly have forgotten. The moment was truly something to behold. For anyone who had never personally witnessed the eruption which accompanied the Anthem, it could not adequately be described in words. It was a combination of the noise of a jet airplane taking off, the cannon blasts from the chorus of the *1812 Overture* and the Fourth of July fireworks display all rolled into one.

People would constantly ask me what it was like to sing the Anthem at the Blackhawks games and I would say, "As great as you say it was to be there... just imagine the feeling of being the guy who is singing." It was truly awesome. The couple minutes of amazing energy surrounding the patriotic fervor all began in 1985, to answer the second-most-often Blackhawks-related question which I was frequently asked.

It was Game 3 of the Campbell Conference Finals series with the Edmonton Oilers, led by The Great One, Wayne Gretzky. He and his teammates had taken the first two games of the best of seven series on their home ice and the experts predicted that the Chicago locals would fall down and die, according to most hockey writers.

Well, they didn't. Fans simply would not let them. Following the singing of O, Canada, the building erupted with sound, later measured at 110 decibels, louder than a jet plane taking off. The spontaneous burst from the voices of the fans was a battle cry loud enough to inspire the dead. It worked. The 'Hawks skated with such intensity and purpose that they could not lose. They won that night and then they won again after an identical overture in Game 4. A tradition had been born.

From that point on, game after game, night after night, the rafters would shake as the powerful Barton Theater Organ would start off the ceremony with an eight-bar introduction, followed by the song that became my trademark, namely, our National Anthem. I once commented that in The Stadium, even communists get goosebumps during the National Anthem. In fact, I suggested that the Marines should set up a recruiting station in the lobby and sign up new recruits right after the Anthem was sung.

There were so many great moments to recall during my tenure with the Blackhawks, I could not possibly capture them all. However, I vividly remember one of the strangest moments of all time. I had finished singing "the tune," as I

54

sometimes call it, when I was hit squarely in the back of the head by a puck that had careened off the crossbar and ricocheted into the organ loft where it found the bullseye in the back of my skull.

Luckily, I was holding on to the guardrail of the rather treacherous steps down to the mezzanine, or I may have dropped to my knees. My first reaction was, "Somebody threw a bottle. Somebody who doesn't like all the noise during the anthem," I thought, even though I'd never heard anything break. The puck hit me flush in the back of the head. Still stunned, I looked up to see an energetic young fan leaning over the front row of the first balcony, who promptly asked, "Hey, Wayne, do you want that puck?" "Yes, I want it," I said. The thing had nearly put a hole in my head. If it hadn't hurt so much, I probably would have burst out laughing at the question.

The most memorable moment in Chicago Stadium that most every fan in Chicago – and many others across North America recall. And the number one memory that people love to ask me about, came on January 19, 1991.

It was a Saturday afternoon the Chicago Stadium was decked out in its finest. It was the NHL All-Star Game, an event of considerable significance. The spectacle was made even grander during the timing of what was happening thousands of miles away from the game. The 42nd National Hockey League All-Star Game was to be staged just a day-and-a-half after the order was given to launch Operation Desert Storm, which later became known as the Persian Gulf War. The real "Madhouse on Madison" was on display for the entire nation to see. It was a day of destiny. A day considered by Chicago sports fans and many followers of the NHL as one of the greatest moments in the history of this great sport.

Again, I was blessed to be chosen to be in that spotlight. There were banners, flags, posters and a crowd of people whose emotions were at fever-pitch. Their messages were honest, their signs were handmade with phrases such as, "No flag burners here," or, "The G.I.'s, the Real All-Stars." It was an inspiring moment of true patriotism and national loyalty that could never be artificially manufactured or duplicated.

Later that month, Super Bowl XXV promoters handed out pre-printed cards to fans as they entered Tampa Stadium and instructed everyone to make noise as Whitney Houston lip-synced to a recording of her own voice singing the National Anthem. That, too, was a great moment, but I will always contend that the Chicago Stadium on that one glorious Saturday afternoon, two weeks earlier in January of 1991, was the real thing.

NBC and the NHL had decided that the Canadian and U.S. Anthems would be carried in their entirety, uninterrupted, no matter what. The director was told he could cut away from game action at any time to air a Gulf War update, but the Anthems were not to be disturbed. Hearing this directive well before the game made me realize what a tremendous responsibility I was being assigned. I thanked God for the talent to do the job and for the confidence to know I was ready for the challenge.

The evening prior to the All-Star Game was the NHL Skills Competition and the Old Timers Exhibition Game where some of the former greats of the NHL put on a show for the fans. The National Anthem for that evening was an experience that many in attendance claim was even more emotional. On that Friday night, there were no TV cameras, no hoards of national media staring at the crowd. It was just pure emotion of the genuine Blackhawks fans who cheered with a sincere wave of patriotism for the country we all so dearly respected.

It was a love affair for a minute-and-a-half with Uncle Sam, apple pie and all things near and dear to us as Americans. As the national TV audience watched the telecast of All-Star Saturday, I recall the countless parades; the Memorial Days, Fourths of July, Veterans Days and all of the National Anthems I had ever sung before in my life. It was a vivid reflection of where I felt my destiny had placed me; precisely in the spot at that moment to do what my God-given talents would allow me to do well. I couldn't help but smile.

I felt as if I were the anchorman of the Olympic Relay Team. I imagined the runner ahead of me approaching with the baton and I knew what had to be accomplished. That one set of National Anthems, above all others at Chicago Stadium, stood out most brilliantly in my memory. I sang it for every man and woman who had ever honored our country by dutifully wearing the uniform of the armed forces. It was sung for the citizens of the small towns across America who had never seen a crowd as large as the one buzzing with energy below and above me from my position in the organ loft on the west end of this marvelous palace of sports and entertainment. I thought about the brave men and women who had given their lives so that we could peacefully assemble to show this spirited pride for our nation.

I prayed for those whose lives were in danger by the latest military action that had all of us frightened and concerned. I felt the pressure to perform well. The kind of pressure a true professional welcomes and responds to. It was a period of just five minutes in my life, yet it was a snapshot in time in our history that I would not trade at any price.

Harvey Wittenberg, the longtime Stadium announcer for the Blackhawks, began his customary monotone introduction and the moment began.

For the national viewing audience, the crowd's response was something many of them had never seen, nor heard before. I knew that it was the traditional outburst that had become the signature of our well-choreographed number in Chicago. But I wasn't about to spoil the illusion. It was showtime, as I loved to call it. The moment when the gathered throng turned their full attention to the organ loft as they waited in anticipation for their leader of song to light the torch. From the far-reaching provinces to the gleaming urban centers, I felt the eyes and ears of the Canadian citizenry turning their attention to me to hear their beloved *O, Canada* sung the way it was meant to be sung, with great pride.

As I reared back and let the music soar with every ounce of energy that my baritone voice could produce, I visualized filling the homes of the loggers in British Columbia, the crowded sports bars of Toronto and all points and Provinces in between with the proud strains of this beautiful anthem.

O Canada, our home and native land. True patriot love in all thy sons* command. With glowing hearts, we see thee rise. The true north, strong and free. From far and wide, O Canada, we stand on guard for thee. God, keep our land glorious and free. O Canada, we stand on guard for thee. O Canada, we stand on guard for thee.

*The lyrics have since been modified to be gender neutral with the phrase, *True patriot love for all of us command.*

I had taken to the baton and ran with it. Carrying with me the maple leaf and all its glory. Once in full stride, The *Star Spangled Banner* that followed immediately was nothing short of pure love set to music. These moments now seemed so long ago and so very far away as I wondered if the opportunity to fill any stadium with my voice would ever present itself to me again. It was a question to which I feared the answer.

Teen Charged With Attempted Murder in Messmer Shooting

--The Daily Herald

"The mere sense of living is joy enough"
--Emily Dickenson

No Fun:

Messmer Shooting Dampens Plans For Chicago Stadium Fete

--The St Louis Post-Dispatch

"The price one pays for pursuing any profession, or calling, is an intimate knowledge of its ugly side."
--James Baldwin

Chapter 5

Looking in the Mirror for Answers

Saturday, April 16, 1994

Wow! I got the first glance at myself in the mirror since the shooting. Let's just say that I had seen better days. In fact, I recall seeing better faces in horror films. The initial reaction was less than favorable. I had an incision from almost ear to ear. So much for vanity at this point. Thank God for a sense of humor. I amused myself by thinking about ringing the nurses' station to see if they could possibly have someone fit me for the bolts in my neck to complete the Frankenstein look. Pity didn't wear well at this time.

It was fairly obvious that I would have some long-term healing to do after the shooting and the surgery. I still felt the need to pray for inner peace. I was hurt and angry. I just wanted to punch something or someone. I laughed as I thought of the phrase that I had used so many times before. "I have a face for radio." Unfortunately, after getting a closer look at the damage, I thought that was a very true statement.

The joke triggered a flashback to one of the happiest periods of my life; the years I had spent on-the-air. I was a radio guy through and through. The thousands of hours spent behind the microphone were flashing before my eyes as if they were yesterday.

Ever since I was a child, radio had fascinated me. My favorite memories involved listening to baseball games broadcast from the west coast when the Cubs would play the

Dodgers or the Giants long before the Padres landed in San Diego. To me, the sounds of summer were the voices of Vince Lloyd and Lou Boudreau on WGN. Before then, my chosen voices of summer were Blaine Walsh and Earl Gillespie calling the play-by-play of my beloved Milwaukee Braves. These were the sounds that enriched my childhood and occupied the wonder years while I filled the endless hours of my boyhood.

If it was a summer day or night, then surely there was baseball on my nine-volt AM-only transistor radio to keep me company in the motionless days of youth where I spent many endless summer nights at my grandparents' house in Southeastern Wisconsin. The magic of the medium was never lost on me. Although I had come along years after the golden age of radio had faded to second-class citizenship status behind television, I always knew there was something quite special about radio.

Perhaps it was the most basic of its attractions that captured my attention. As a young boy, I was never one to waste words, carefully choosing the times that I spoke. Radio allowed me the creative freedom to provide my own pictures to accompany the words that I heard, having a vivid imagination. I suppose now that radio and its theater of the mind magic was always the perfect fit for me.

When the "Old Commander" Bob Elson said, "A swing and a slow ball... and a miss," describing the Go-Go White Sox in 1959, I pictured every spin of the laces as the ball passed the frustrated batsman, who had just taken a futile swipe at the elusive sphere. Elson's partner in the booth was another person who would ultimately win a place in my heart. Milo Hamilton. He was another in a long list of Iowa Hawkeyes who went on to prominence and a Hall of Fame broadcasting career at that. With the duo of Bob Elson and Milo Hamilton at work from Comiskey Park and all ports of call in the American League, I grew to love the sounds of the game almost as dearly as the game itself and the names that came with it.

Ballgames on the radio left a great impression on me as a young kid from Chicago's South Side. The two broadcasters whom I admired the most were Vince Lloyd and the great Jack Quinlan, both of whom I was convinced were aware that I was listening on every pitch. Quinlan was colorful, clever and very witty. He made some miserable Cubs teams of the early 1960's actually sound exciting, despite their on-field performances.

I remember hearing the news of his death in March of 1965 in an auto accident in Scottsdale, Arizona during one spoiled Spring Training. I felt as though I'd lost a true friend. Another Cubs' tragedy around the same period was the loss of Kenny Hubbs, the talented second baseman who had captured the National League Rookie of the Year honors in 1962. He was a player of promise and hope for the Cubs fans to rally around. Everyone in baseball fully expected that Hubbs was destined to be the second baseman for many years to come. I also vividly remember the newscast broadcasting the breaking story of Hubbs' death in a plane crash just prior to the 1964 season.

I was playing in my backyard at the time, probably staging a one-man version of a World Series Game when I stopped cold in my tracks. I remember feeling the emptiness, the loss of a person from my world of baseball whom I admired. Ken Hubbs was a ball player that the great Lou Boudreau, surely would have described as a "good kid."

The magic of radio had also brought me to another great sports moment. The famed Floyd Patterson versus Ingemar Johansson heavyweight title fights captured my utmost attention. I followed the blow-by-blow of the would-be champions and they pummeled each other with a ferocity that could be felt right through the blaring 12-inch speaker that I was huddled around. I remember positioning myself on the dining room floor, just inches from the console radio to hear the series of fights. It was wonderful. It was radio, and I loved it.

It was in the same dining room, not more than a few years later, when I cheered the Chicago Bears on to victory as they captured the world championship in a thrilling victory over Frank Gifford's New York Giants on a chilly Sunday afternoon in 1963, with Jack Quinlan at the mic. I busied myself with a homework assignment at the dining room table as I cheered on the Monsters of the Midway to the crown. Again, radio was there as my best companion. Somehow and in some fashion, I wanted to be a part of that magical world.

The radio business first started tugging at my sleeve while I was an undergraduate at Illinois Wesleyan University in downstate Bloomington. Majoring in Music Education, I discovered a fondness and appreciation of different kinds of music. The campus radio station went on the air during the spring of my senior year. I missed the chance to be a part of the new station by a few months, although it made me hungry for the experience.

Despite having the interest, the opportunity to pursue a broadcasting job didn't present itself until a few years after graduation when I had returned to Chicago. If I was going to be honest with myself and practice what I preach when I speak to young people, I would have to at least try to do what I love to do as often as I could possibly do it. I always felt that when you followed your passion, eventually your performances would catch up with your enthusiasm.

This was the case with radio. I was told that if I wanted to be on the air in Chicago, I would have to find a job in some small town and then, after a few years, I could possibly work my way back to the big city. That was someone else's path. It wasn't what I envisioned for my career. In radio, jobs are one won through constantly barraging program directors with audition tapes and resumes, just like any other numbers game. The more you hand out, the better your odds are. That is, assuming that you have the talent.

The trouble is, there's always someone who is willing to work for less and the guys doing the hiring know that. After all, they started at the bottom too. It is an easy job search to give up on. I refused to quit. With a simple attitude adjustment, I recall taking a positive frame of mind, which made a huge difference. When I was told "no," I didn't hear the word "no" as a rejection. I heard, "Not now," or, "Not here." I discovered that when you change your attitude, you change your life. My attitude was not one of defeat, but rather one of determination. I repeatedly told myself that I needed to work harder and to continue to believe in my dream.

When I was notified of another rejection, I said to myself, "I'm sorry, Mr. Program Director, but you won't be there with me to share in my success." Of course, I didn't say that out loud or I would have never gotten my first job. It was amazing what a little attitude adjustment did back then. Opportunities had been plentiful, although slow in coming. My first professional radio experience was actually a blessing in many ways. WXFM Radio in Chicago was very much like the station portrayed on the old television program WKRP in Cincinnati. A handful of colorful characters showed up every day to play radio.

The absentee station owner often appeared without advanced notice, dropping in from his home in Switzerland to count his money and stir things up a bit. Robert Victor had purchased the station for a few hundred thousand dollars several years before my arrival on the scene in 1975. He subsequently sold his ownership in the station for $10 million to a corporate broadcasting company who quickly dismantled and reassembled a station of their own. They replaced everything but the dial frequency – 105.9 FM.

Since joining WXFM 106, I had gradually worked my way up from my original assignment of reading weather forecasts and station identification between foreign language programs and the live church service remote broadcasts, earning a spot as a staff announcer. I took over the overnight slot from a veteran broadcaster who had moved to another Chicago station. All of those years playing in the French horn sections of orchestras and bands finally paid off when I was offered the opportunity to host the all-night classical music program known as Nightcap, from midnight to 6:00 a.m.

I selected a rather lush version of the classic melody of Stella By Starlight as my theme. I launched into the late night and early morning hours as the friendly companion voice for classical music-loving insomniacs. But just because I had my show did not mean I had it easy. After hosting my overnight program, I would then have to be the morning newscaster as well. At about $6.50 an hour, I needed to string together some time on the clock in order to make a living wage. So I didn't complain. I would not trade the experience for twice the $10 an hour I would soon command as a season's professional broadcaster. Being at the right place at the right time started to be something I had crafted into an art form.

A well-meaning but not terribly talented man had been brokering time for the morning show. He played a collection of vintage radio shows from the 1930s and '40s and made some comments between the programs. I was his engineer, running the control board and helping out wherever I could.

Finally, finances ran out and the station owner canceled his show.

Having missed the glory days of radio, I had gained an appreciation for the period of radio's heyday through my experience over the past couple of years. When I was asked if I knew the old radio shows well enough to host and program a show by myself, I responded, "Sure I do." That's why I pursued the radio dream in the first place; to eventually have my own program and here was an opportunity being dropped in my lap.

For three years, I became intimately familiar with the programs of Fibber McGee and Molly, Jack Benny, Amos and Andy, Eddie Cantor, Al Jolson and a host of other great stars from when radio was king. It was always a work in progress as I continued to learn as much as I could about the entertainment world of that period and of radio itself. The shows were fun to listen to and even more fun to share with other people who appreciated them.

I gained valuable experience as the host and producer of the WXFM 106 Old Time Radio Show. This three-year run was fun while it lasted, but ultimately gave way to a year of working with one of the great early TV pioneers, who had moved to Chicago from New York to do a radio show on our station. His name was Claude Kirchner. He was a classic.

Claude emerged on the TV scene at a time when no more than a handful of families on any given block actually had a TV set. He was the ringmaster for TV's first three-ring entertainment variety show called Super Circus in the early 1950s. The program thrilled children of all ages from a live broadcast at the Civic Theater in Chicago's famed Opera House. From there, it was telecast nationwide via the ABC Television Network.

Claude paved the way for others who were to follow him and cohost Mary Hartline as they thrilled the kids fortunate enough to watch them entertain on a black and white screen, keeping them company in between bites of peanut butter and jelly sandwiches.

The Claude Kirchner who I came to know was as sweet as any person I had ever met. But his time in the spotlight as a program host had dimmed quite considerably before his arrival at WXFM. As the old ringmaster took his final bow, his exit opened yet another door for me. When I took over the morning show and evolved it into a music program, it became a blend of standards, big band and jazz music, coupled with some hometown personality. It was a formula that apparently worked well enough for people to still make comments to me about having listened to the show many years later, long after the show and the station went off the air.

When WXFM finally did pull the plug on the jazz format into which it had evolved, the new sound of WAGO – or G106 – took the airwaves as a top 40 station. Overnight, I found myself as the sports director of Chicago's newest radio station. G106, by historical standards, was a bust. It lasted for exactly one year. I recall the morning we changed formats. It was my 6:00 a.m. sportscast where the new call letters were heard for the first time. "With the sports, I'm Wayne Messmer on WCKG," I said proudly, announcing the even newer, new kid on the radio block.

The wildest ride of my radio life was when I was part of a morning show on WYTZ. Better known to the ranks of listeners as Z95. It was a whirlwind of activity known as the Barsky Morning Zoo. I had been brought in to do the news and sports with a personality. I was teamed with Paul Barsky and Kit Paraventi, a couple of comedic characters from out of town. Once again, my local identity was my greatest asset, along with a pretty good radio voice.

Paul had been brought in from Philadelphia, while Kit had most recently been on the air in Detroit. Somehow, we found each other in the same studio early on weekday mornings, challenged with trying to entertain the masses during Chicago's drive time. The trio was eventually pared down to the duo of Paul and me. The team of Barsky and Wayne enjoyed a wave of popularity that provided nonstop fun for us and for the listening audience for over three years. The ratings, the livelihood of the radio world, were great, but the cruelty of the industry showed itself when Paul was abruptly fired following a Friday morning program.

An operations director who simply didn't like Barsky anymore effectively killed one of the most popular radio programs and radio stations in the city. This programming genius was himself later fired because of sagging ratings following Paul's dismissal. Times changed after that and so did my opinion of the radio industry, proving once again that being in the right place at the right time was becoming a way of life for me. I made the move to our sister station, WLS, when a position opened up in the news department.

Now a serious newscaster instead of a news sidekick, I found myself on the midday news shift at one of America's great radio stations. I wrote and delivered the local newscasts during the hourly breaks of the Rush Limbaugh Show for the listening audience throughout mid-America. This was quite a departure from all of the silliness I had been a part of earlier in my radio career.

I had come to accept as truth the analogy that a radio career was similar to standing on the shore at a beach as the ocean waves were crashing behind you. You could hear the force of the waves rumbling in and you knew that sooner or later, one wave would ultimately take you down and, maybe, take you under. You never knew which one or how hard it would hit or when it would get you, but you knew it was coming. The only certainty in the radio industry is that it will constantly be changing. This constant state of motion will, unfortunately, swallow even the innocent at times.

I left WLS after three years during a period of budget readjustment. I never figured my radio career was over for good, but as I reflected on the thousands of hours spent at the microphone, I was in a hospital bed with a tracheostomy tube sticking out of my throat, fairly certain that those days had sadly ended with the cruel irony of having been shot in the throat. It was a wonderful and exciting roller coaster ride that fearfully had ended all too soon and for the wrong reason.

Singer shot after hockey game

--The Denver Rocky Mountain News

"Anyone who says something is impossible, is always interrupted by someone doing it"
--Anonymous

Without Messmer, Stadium Is Cold And Empty Place

--The Chicago Sun-Times

"The National Anthem was written
with Wayne Messmer in mind"
--Gary C., Chicago Hockey Fan

Chapter 6
Letter to a Friend

Sunday, April 17, 1994
3:22 a.m.

My Dear Friend,

I'm trying to piece together a few things that have happened to me over the past week and I need an ear. You kept coming to mind as the right guy, so please bear with me in these late-night ramblings of a troubled man.

I've always admired and respected your sense of priorities and commitment to your family, which is why I hope this letter will make sense. I'm worried about what parents will say when their children ask, "What happened to the guy who sings the Anthem?" The answer must be more than just, "He got shot," which, trust me, is frightening enough for a child to hear. But more needs to be said. The problem is, how do you say it in a way a child will understand and not be terrified?

Man to man, I will share with you the personal nightmare of my life, which has become my world since last week. I now operate with a tube attached to my chest so that I can eat. I constantly have to sit up to have my bandages changed for the tracheostomy tube in my throat that allows me to breathe. Mostly, I am shaking with fear that I will possibly never speak again. I cannot even consider the possibility of singing.

It all seems so impossible at this point. Getting shot has really derailed me. I keep wondering what it was that I did wrong. I did not knowingly put myself in undue danger. I did not pick a fight. I did not fail to look both ways before crossing the street. I did not forget to buckle my seatbelt. The answer to why this happened is slow in coming. I did nothing wrong. I did not cause this to happen. Knowing that makes me think that it just isn't fair.

So how do parents tell their children that even when you do all the things you are told, bad things still sometimes happen? I don't want to send a message to children that if you obey your parents, eat your spinach and follow the rules, et cetera, that life sometimes will still occasionally bring some unwanted surprises.

I'm very angry right now, but I don't know how to defuse it. The biggest need I have at this time is for understanding and support. I need a friend to be able to talk to. I decided that I would need an ally as I draw up the battle plans to continue with my future. I would hope that I can count on you. I don't want to turn into a person who dwells on his misfortune, making everyone around him feel uncomfortable. I want to make sure that impressionable young people aren't told a story about a guy who didn't do anything wrong, but got shot anyway. I don't want the responsibility of frightening any kids with the details of my story.

If there was any way to avoid letting a senseless random act of violence steal a huge portion of my life, I owe it to myself, to Kathleen and to the thousands of well-wishers who have rallied behind me in hopes of a happy ending to this saga to try as hard as I possibly can to recover.

I'm approaching every new day with caution and a sense of forced patience. The point is, my friend, I'll be back. And when I am, I may need some guidance and support if the final chapter of this experience stops short of the proverbial happy ending.

Thanks for listening. It means a lot.

Wayne

For the record, The "Dear Friend" letter was written to my friend and broadcasting colleague Steve Dahl.

2nd Suspect Arrested In Messmer Shooting

--The Chicago Sun-Times

"Life is what happens while you're busy making other plans."
--John Lennon

Messmer Tape Will Rock Stadium

--The Chicago Sun-Times

"The longer I live, the more beautiful life becomes."
--Frank Lloyd Wright

Chapter 7

The Guy Who Used to Sing the Anthem

Monday, April 18, 1994

The day began after a long night of coughing and choking. I was pleased with the fact that the weekend was over, if for no other reason than the weekend nursing crew was less familiar to me than the regular weekday full-time staff.

I was optimistic, but cautious, as Dr. Harold Pelzer entered my room for a 7:00 a.m. consultation. He was the specialist in whom I was counting to tell me the truth about what it might take to try and get past my present condition. Dr. Pelzer had a quiet and very calm personality, which helped to ease some of the anxiety surrounding the rest of my world as it had erupted before me. I welcomed his visits and his conversations since they were spoken in a reassuring tone of voice that implied, even if it were not intentional, that everything was going to work out.

I prayed to hear him say those words. Today would not be the day when I would hear them. His comments, as they had been in the past, were centered on facts and not disguised with speculation. While the doctor failed to give me a definite answer, it seemed as though a lot of people had already signed me up for the church choir to start at the end of the month. Kathleen remained cautiously, but realistically, optimistic; providing a daily dose of motivation.

Meanwhile, I was still anxiously waiting to grunt a sound of any kind. Before Dr. Pelzer could talk about the plans for the day, his four assistants swooped in and removed the two remaining drains from the massive incision in my throat. I must admit that while the procedure was less than comfortable, the idea of moving toward recovery was enough to make me grin and bear it.

After they had removed the two drains, it was time to take out the stitches – somewhere in the neighborhood of 15 to 20 across the front of my neck. All I could think about was the enormous scar I would probably have when this was all over. I imagined little children spotting me in line for the freak show in the carnival and starting to scream.

Again, as with the drains, despite the pricking and pulling sensation by the pair of surgeons who have hovered over my throat, I knew that the pain was worth it. The schedule for the rest of the day included an actual visit to Dr. Pelzer's office in an adjoining building in the hospital complex. Also on tap was the cookie test, which was still tops on my to-do list.

The cookie test was a rather strange procedure where doctors would monitor and x-ray image of my head and throat while I chewed and swallowed a cookie. They were checking the operating efficiency of my swallowing mechanism. I was totally determined to pass the test. "Small hurdles first," I told myself over and over again.

Tuesday, April 19, 1994

Let's hear it for the boy! I passed the cookie test with flying colors. It meant that when I swallowed, everything went down the right pipe. To me, this was a giant leap forward. The troops were rejoicing and so was I, but I felt it was considerably premature. "There is a voice!" comes the cry from the camp and, "There will be one," says John Marquart, MD, who visited the room last night carrying good news. "I'm not sure whether you will end up as a bass, tenor, alto or a soprano," he said to me as my family members gathered around the bedside of the battle-scarred warrior. "It could take two months, four months or even six months, but it will come back," the good doctor proclaimed.

I was encouraged by the news. I wished that I was able to share his enthusiasm and his confidence. No one else had offered such a bold prognosis. At least not within earshot of me. "What will come back?" I grunted from the tracheostomy tube, size 6, to be downsized tomorrow to size 4. It's great news, sure, but there are still a lot of questions to be answered. Speculation to deal with and facts of reality still looking me in the face.

The nagging question on my list of concerns is, "Will I sound the same?" Actually, different is okay too, I told myself. I just needed to know something. Although I reminded myself once more what had happened just slightly over a week ago, I was still aware that I had already won the first battle of this war: the fight to stay alive.

By the end of the day, the tide had turned. I'd made some audible sounds, although they sounded froggy and hoarse. But I appreciated the fact that I was not using pen and paper anymore to communicate. And, to make things even better, it was finally time to try some food. After all, I had aced the now famous cookie test. Tasteless jello, bland tea and a rather unusual smelling soup broth where the best that they could do to reacquaint me to the world of real food. The prescribed diet of clear liquids was not something you would select from a four-star menu, but to me it was as welcome as a filet cooked to perfection. That was breakfast.

Not to my surprise, I had the exact same meal for lunch. And, to add even more salt to the wound, it was dinner too. My evening's meal was interrupted just long enough to downsize the tracheostomy tube from a size six to a size four. I also had the central IV line removed, which separated me from the IV tree for the first time in 11 days. I celebrated with a walk to the elevators with Kathleen and my sister, Barb, who was in Chicago from Albuquerque, NM to be with me.

We went long enough to meet a couple dear friends who were coming to visit. The whole group brought a great deal of cheer to the room and when they finally did go home, I could sense the love they left behind. I was still not ready to put on the party hat, but I was pleased with the fact that I now felt my list of life's options had been increased. Regardless of the quality of improvement from this point on, at least I would be able to speak and that, to me, meant hope.

As a highlight of the day, I pick up the phone and call my mom and dad at home before they came to visit. It was a phone call that I will never forget, and neither would they. As my mother picked up the phone, I simply spoke one word, "Mama," I said in a rough-sounding, but recognizable voice. Her response was absolute joy. She had heard her boy speak again. I spoke very little that night, not because I was uncomfortable or in pain, but rather I was filled with the anticipation of the next day's arrival. I could sense the feeling of hope growing inside me.

Daybreak came, and I was without the aid of the tubes and pumps for the first time in a dozen days. The independence was something that I was very anxious to try out. I kept thinking more and more about the gift of my voice as it was shared and now as it had been stolen. My focus had now shifted almost entirely on my efforts to get it back. Knowing that the talent was God-given, I also realized that it had been my choice to use it, trying to make a difference. I reaffirmed my choice to share and cultivate my gift rather than choosing to hoard it. I wanted to be able to share whatever new gifts I would be given as part of this life challenge.

I wanted the opportunity to tell the story of a person who believed in himself and his abilities to as many people as were willing to listen. I wanted to convey a simple story of keeping hope alive. It suddenly seemed vitally important to me to tell others how hard I had to work to put myself in a place where being in the right place at the right time just seemed to happen. I recognized how very fortunate I had been to have had the experiences I had enjoyed through the years, trying not to be selfish. I knew that if it all ended right here, I still had been abundantly blessed with wonderful opportunities. Yet, I still set my sights high.

I thought about the thousands of talented and very deserving individuals who never had one-hundredth of the chances I had to have been at center court, in the organ loft, at center ice, at home plate, in the booth. "It had been a tremendous career, even if it ends here right now," I told myself sternly, hoping that this was not the case.

One thing I could not keep from thinking about was the legacy of Wayne Messmer. What would I leave behind as the guy who used to sing the Anthem? I tried to imagine it, but I couldn't help to think back to another era in my life when it all began so innocently. Having completed my assigned duties of reading the hourly weather forecast, I grabbed my coat and headed to the elevator and down from the 34th floor to the 15th floor of the famed 333 North Michigan Avenue Building.

I had been a staff announcer at WXFM Radio for five years already by the time I was able to enjoy the Christmas lights sparkling throughout the city from my radio studio perspective on the uppermost floor of this landmark building. As a regular part of my daily routine, I enjoyed a spectacular view, directly up the "Magnificent Mile" of historic Michigan Avenue, looking toward the iconic Chicago Water Tower, several blocks North.

The destination was a Christmas party being thrown by the Chicago Sting Soccer Team. I was excited to meet the guys and the rest of the front office staff who would be there. Never did I realize that I was crossing the threshold of an entirely new chapter in my life.

WXFM was the flagship station of the Chicago Sting Soccer Team and I was thrilled to be part of the station broadcasting the games. It was new, exciting and fresh. It was all part of the fun of being in the world of radio and sports. At the party, I wondered out loud, "Who sings the Anthem for your games?" The account executive for the ad agency representing the team told me, "No one in particular."

Having put one foot firmly inside the door, I made the push to volunteer my services for the occasion. I purposely kept it to myself that I had been trained as a singer and stage performer. To this day, I still think they figured I would be just another in a long line of radio DJs who think they can sing and then go about the business of trying to painfully convince everyone else.

After a little more conversation, I said, "I'm not kidding," and I was able to secure a formal invitation to come out to Chicago Stadium for an indoor Soccer match in late November 1980 to show what I could do. I was very excited.

It was great to think that I would get the chance to sing at a professional sporting event. Of course, I didn't know then that it would be the first of thousands of such appearances. To me, the first was certainly most thrilling,

84

simply because of the potential it offered for the future. Needless to say, I had marked the calendar and readied myself for the highly anticipated debut at Chicago Stadium.

As it turned out, it was even more fun than I imagined it would be. The crowd was alive with excitement. It was the newly introduced sport of indoor soccer and The Sting was a big success. They did a tremendous job of dressing up the building to make it an entertainment event, not just another game. Following my introduction, I was handed the microphone, which appeared to be circa 1957. I thought it was probably the same one that had been used at famous prize fights and political rallies through the years in this famous building that had been the home for so many historic occasions.

Microphone in hand and cord in tow, I walked out onto the carpeted playing surface and belted out the strains of Irving Berlin's, God Bless America which was selected as the song of choice as a personal favorite of the team owner, Lee Stern. I will never forget the crowd's reaction. For any performer, the sound of applause is an elixir. It makes you want to continue to sing so that the applause won't ever stop. It was a special moment of which dreams are made. I was proud to be there. Proud to be an American and certainly proud to be able to share the gift of my voice.

The Sting front office personnel were impressed by the performance. They were so pleased that I was immediately invited back for an encore, an invitation I instantly accepted. Following the second appearance, the team's Executive Vice President offered me the position as the permanent soloist. I loved the idea. Of course, I immediately took him up on the offer.

The Sting games were quickly becoming one of my favorite leisure activities and I was rapidly evolving into a major fan of the team, as well as the sport they played. Seizing the opportunity was a very rewarding feeling, one that I knew I wanted to duplicate.

When presented with the chance to sing at every game, the issue of compensation was brought up. I worked out the big money deal and it was determined that I would be paid an impressive $25 a game for services rendered. Along with the package, I would get free parking, a free meal and four tickets. A great deal, I thought, without any heavy lifting. It was going to be fun. It already was! The folks at the radio station were impressed with the singing and with my ability to self-promote.

While The Sting were pleased to have found a guy who could bring something extra to the table, as someone in the front office commented, the best part of it all was that I could always use a couple extra bucks anyway and I could think of no better way to earn a few dollars than by combining two of my favorite activities, music and sports.

An even bigger break came when the team's Director of Communications called me to see if I would be interested in working as the fill-in public address announcer for the Chicago radio sportscaster who was doing it at the time. Without missing a beat, I jumped at the chance. Although I recognized that there was a small problem: I really didn't know much about the sport, but I was willing to learn fast.

While I had been at the games and had enjoyed them, I was not terribly familiar with the rules of indoor soccer and even less familiar with the terms used to describe them. When asked if I thought I knew the game well enough to handle an assignment, I responded with a confident, "Of course I do. I love the game," as if I'd grown up playing it.

True, I did love the game, but my only exposure had been the few games I watched at Chicago Stadium after singing. "Oh well," I thought. "It's time to do some homework." Sensing the bigger picture, I got down to the business of boning up on the world's most popular sport. Armed with my newfound knowledge, I arrived at the game that following Saturday afternoon ready to get down to business. Apparently, it worked. At halftime, a couple of the staffers came up to me in the announcer's position in the press box and told me that I had "impressed the right people," with my performance.

Two days later, at the weekly media luncheon, in the midst of a question and answer session with the press, I was handed a business card with a message inscribed in the back, "How would you like to do the PA for our outdoor season?" Again, it took me no time to think about it and responded with a firm, "Yes, of course. I'd love it." We shook hands and agreed to work out the details later.

The Sting were in their first season of playing indoor soccer, the Americanized version of the sport, although they had been playing the traditional outdoor game since the inception of the franchise as a member of the North American Soccer League in 1975. The bigger question was, did I know the intricacies of the outdoor game? Once again, I rewound the tape and spoke the answer that they wanted to hear. "Of course I know the game. I love it." This time, I was really stretching the truth. In fact, I stretched it so far that it nearly came back to slap me in the face.

The only outdoor soccer match I had ever seen in my entire life was in Guadalajara, Mexico and my recollections of that contest were more related to the excitement of the stadium and the crowd than with the game. That, coupled with the fact that I was an American fan in the midst of a Spanish-speaking crowd left me with a slightly less than the full grasp that I would have preferred to draw upon for my experiential reference. In short, I need to do some more homework.

Fortunately, there was enough time to learn what I needed to know. The lexicon was not as difficult as I had initially feared. Day after day, as the season came closer, I continued to cram soccer knowledge. It was then that I adopted the phrase, "Why embarrass yourself in public if you don't have to?" I still regularly ask the same question.

Somehow, I strung together enough words and phrases to be ready to assume the role of Public Address Announcer for the Chicago Sting on opening day in April, 1981. The exposure of singing at Chicago Stadium had paid off handsomely for me.

At the conclusion of the 1980-81 Sting indoor season, I received a call from the part-time publicist for the Chicago Blackhawks. He asked if I would be interested in coming out to sing the National Anthem for the final regular season game of the year against the St. Louis Blues. Once again, the answer was an immediate yes. I couldn't wait for the chance to sing for a hockey game. This was my team! The Blackhawks. It was Bobby Hull, Stan Mikita and Glen Hall, who were the heroes of my childhood. They captured my heart as a kid and had continued to keep me as a fan well into adulthood. I knew I would enjoy the experience.

The phenomenon grew during the summer of 1981 as The Sting continued to gain fan momentum and support. The team featured the great Karl-Heinz Granitza and a collection of European and American stars. They captured the hearts of the city by doing what Chicago fans love best: winning. The Sting battled their way through the season on the field, playing well enough to earn their way to Soccer Bowl '81 and the Championship Game in Toronto. They made it there by scoring a dramatic shootout victory over the

San Diego Sockers before more than 40,000 delirious fans at Comiskey Park on a memorable misty night in late September.

The team's popularity was aided by the Major League Baseball strike, which left The Sting as the showcase team of the city. When The Sting brought the Championship trophy back to Chicago, they were welcomed with a ticker tape parade down LaSalle Street and a rally at the Daley Center. This was no small accomplishment. The year was 1981. It was the first title the Windy City had seen in any professional sport since the Chicago Bears of 1963. This was long before the Bulls began their perennial championship runs or the White Sox and the Cubs had won their respective Division Titles and subsequent World Series. Yes, it was still years away from the Bears' Super Bowl XX victory in January of 1986.

With all the attention for The Sting, a lot of fans heard me sing at either Wrigley Field or Comiskey Park where The Sting provided the excitement to fill the summer days and nights instead of the striking baseball clubs. I learned during the summer of 1981 that by doing what you love and loving what you do, you can achieve a tremendous level of satisfaction in your life. I made the important discovery that I was a musician first and everything else second. I used my musical training and talents to open new doors.

The Anthem of our beloved country had served me well. I often kiddingly say that I felt a bit guilty about making a career out of singing a song that we all learn in first grade, but apparently I paid more attention than the rest of the kids in class that day.

One question that people ask me all the time is, "What is the favorite National Anthem that you've ever sung?" Certainly the NHL All-Star game was one of the most significant. However, it was a torturously hot afternoon in 1987 in Cooperstown, NY that stands out in my mind as my personal and perhaps my sentimental favorite.

The Cubs and the Cleveland Indians were at Doubleday Field to play an exhibition Hall of Fame game, which used to be played as part of the Baseball Hall of Fame Induction Ceremonies. My unforgettable moment came after being introduced to sing by the great voice of the legendary Yankees' Hall of Fame announcer, Mel Allen. I walked to the microphone, which stood about 20 feet in front of a dozen or so Hall of Famers, who were lined up in front of the pitchers' mound. The mercury had climbed past the 95-degree mark and was still rising, yet I refused to take off my dark blue sport jacket or my tie. This was too serious to be casual, I thought. "This is the Hall of Fame," I told myself with pride.

I remember looking at the faces in the crowd as I filled the air of this quaint upstate New York village with my voice. Young boys were standing at attention, painting an image that would have inspired Norman Rockwell. The youngsters held their baseball caps over their hearts as if to be in on the set design. They didn't hold the caps of modern teams. Instead, they carried the caps of the New York Giants, the Brooklyn Dodgers, the St. Louis Browns. It was as if I had been taken back to a simpler time, when I was eight years old again and had been granted a birthday wish as I blew out the candles on my cake. I knew that I would have wished to be right where I was, and I couldn't believe that it had come true right before my eyes.

After I finished singing, Kathleen and I walked out of the ballpark and toward our seats when I burst into tears. If there had been any doubt just how passionately I felt about being the guy who sings the Anthem, those doubts were completely dashed in those few moments of scorching summer July sun on a ballfield in upstate NY.

Singing the Anthem in that setting, a seemingly simple experience, once again lifted my appreciation of the beauty of the gift that I had given. But that was then, and this was now. The gift was now out of my possession and back to the source where it had originated. I questioned whether I would be given the identical gift twice in my life or whether it would be altered in such a way that I would have to switch to a "Plan B," or possibly a "Plan C." I prayed for answers as I waited for the arrival of a breakfast consisting of something other than tasteless broth, tea and jello. The lesser of my prayers was soon answered, but not to my satisfaction. I shrugged my shoulders when the food tray arrived with the disappointing trio of broth, tea and jello again and I continued to pray for a more significant request.

Special Anthem To Honor Messmer

--The Daily Herald

"Friendship is the only cement that will hold the world together."
--Woodrow Wilson

A Flag For Wayne
--The Chicago Tribune

"The better part of one's life consists of his friendships."
--Abraham Lincoln

Chapter 8

Save Me A Seat In The Bleachers

Wednesday, April 20, 1994

Small things, small favors and little victories began to mean a lot. I appreciated the fact that I felt my prayers were even in a small way being answered. Kathleen was on my mind this morning more than ever. She told me last night that yesterday was the first day she did not wake up crying since all of this happened. The gift may now be our time together. Because of this episode, I planned to maximize the time I spend with my loving wife and terrific daughters.

My sister, Barb, was with me again this morning. We spent some time on the roof at the hospital today actually having a chance to talk about life and the future that is beginning to look brighter by the day. I let my mom and dad have the chance to rejoice with me today. I let down the mood of seriousness long enough to celebrate some of the physical progress I've made, however small. I did this despite the dimness of the light being cast on the big picture.

The Chicago Cubs honored me in a very personal way today, unveiling a banner with my initials – WM – to fly over the roof of the "Friendly Confines" until I can come back as the announcer and/or the singer of the National Anthem. I don't know when that might be, if at all.

It was a most flattering gesture, of which I was enormously grateful. Baseball has been a big part of my life from my early childhood. The privilege to be a part of the

Chicago baseball picture is something that makes me very proud. Our national pastime has provided me with a great deal of joy over the years, both as a fan and as an announcer. I thought back to all the warm summers spent at the ballparks, now silently wondering if all future memories would only be available to me as a fan.

The most vivid image was of that of my last game, now just a couple of weeks ago. It was no different than any of the other hundreds of games for which I had sung and/or announced in the past years. The total was nearing a thousand big league games by then. It was April 7, 1994. The difference on this particular day was that the contest would not count in the standings. This was a game for bragging rights between the Cubs and the White Sox. The "SouthSiders" had their secret weapon in uniform that afternoon. He wore number 45 for baseball, unlike his legendary number 23 when he was on the hardwood court. It was to be Michael Jordan's first and my last appearance at Wrigley Field. At least for a while.

Later, I would think it was fitting that the last game I would work as the Public Address announcer would be a contest between the two ball clubs for whom I had rendered services over the past 13 seasons. There was something rather nostalgic about reading the lineups that afternoon; just saying the words "The Chicago White Sox" over the PA system was a flashback to when I had first started out. It was at historic Comiskey Park – the real one – where I cut my teeth as a PA announcer in 1982.

I remembered getting a message at the WXFM studios that Eddie had called, and he wanted to talk to me. Eddie, was none other than Eddie Einhorn who, along with Jerry Reinsdorf had purchased the White Sox from Bill Veeck and his group a year earlier. Those wonderful South Side summers were loaded with great memories. This was the

95

same ballpark where I had spent much of my early baseball childhood, cheering on the heroes of my generation – Nellie Fox, Luis Aparicio, Moose Skowron, Jim Landis, the slow-footed Sherm Lollar, Early Wynn and, yes, Minnie Minoso.

Here it was, a chilly afternoon in spring on the North Side. The vines in their mid-summer traditional lushness had become a Wrigley Field trademark since the very same Bill Veeck had suggested that they might look good on the brick wall of the bleachers way back in 1937. As for the game itself, it turned out to be even more insignificant and meaningless than I thought possible. The umpires and the teams decided to call it quits with the game tied in extra innings. Nobody won the bragging rights and the unending war between North and South was left unclaimed on the playing field for the remainder of that summer.

I had made sure that I was scheduled to sing the Anthem that day, as I had every other year when the Sox made their trip North. I sang as a gesture of thanks to the guys who gave me my first opportunity in baseball – the White Sox. My three years as field announcer and National Anthem soloist with the Sox were a lot fun. I was very fortunate that in my second year with the team, Tony LaRussa led the boys to an amazing season when they won the Western Division of the American League by 20 games. I could recall the night they clinched it as if it were last night. The Division clinching game in late September of 1983 capped off a dominating season.

The party began with Julio Cruz scampered across the plate with the winning run. It was another in a series of nights when I walked into the parking lot without being able to fully enjoy the fruits of victory. I had a self-imposed curfew because of the morning radio shift that I was working. Although I dreaded having to leave the party early, it was often a blessing to have an excuse to be able to escape a group of post-game revelers before the heavy artillery was rolled out.

To make a good thing even better, Major League Baseball had selected Comiskey Park to host the 1983 All-Star game on July 10 of that year. I would get the chance to announce the lineups and the game itself. This was a dream come true for a South Side kid, who had taken the Archer Avenue bus to 35th street – along with my brother, Bud, and a bunch of our friends – to dozens of games over the years. This was the big time. This was the Major League Baseball All-Star game.

The 50th anniversary MLB All-Star game would be played at the very same location where the concept was born in 1933 when Arch Ward, a *Chicago Tribune* Sports Writer promoted the idea to get the best players in the game together for an exhibition contest. Accounts from the initial All-Star game told of the legend of George Herman "Babe" Ruth, thrilling the crowd with one of his patented home runs. History seemed to live very comfortably at Old Comiskey Park, which was once billed as "The Baseball Palace of the World." It still was as far as I was concerned.

For some reason, recollections of those fun days on the other side of town were swirling about in my head that afternoon as I walked onto the playing surface at beautiful Wrigley Field. Ironically, the first Sox game I had announced actually had a Wrigley Field connection. The Chicago Sting had a soccer match that went into overtime and it was eventually decided in a shootout. I didn't have any time to spare before I had to get down to Comiskey Park for the Sox game.

As fate would have it, the first several games of which I would have made my debut had been snowed out. This forced the schedule maker to start off the Sox with a night doubleheader as the home opener for the 1982 season. Anyone who has ever tried knows that getting from point A – Wrigley Field – to point B – Comiskey Park – during rush hour is a traffic nightmare, a near impossibility. I became an expert at getting from one event to another. I learned a lot of shortcuts over the years in order to balance the practice of constantly booking myself in two places at the same time.

That late afternoon, I arrived at 35th and Shields just in time to make the pre-game announcements and read the lineups. It was not the most relaxed situation I had ever been in. As I burst into the press box, the White Sox Marketing Director was poised at the microphone, ready to start doing the job I had been hired to do. It was obvious that he was upset with the fact that I was arriving just under the wire. But, before long, the dust settled and I was in the flow of the game.

The strange thing about my first day on the job – and virtually every day thereafter – was that I basically taught myself how to do it. No one sat down to talk over things such as style, technique, timing or any of the peculiarities which I eventually developed into a manual for myself with the White Sox and used later with the Cubs. I was a bit uncomfortable taking the chair from an experienced veteran who had held the post for years prior to my importation from the world of soccer, in which, of course, I was now an expert.

After my rather bumpy start, I quickly slid into a comfortable groove. I started to feel at home in the front row of the press box at Old Comiskey Park. Perhaps my best ally during these years was a veteran public relations pro who had also worked both ends of town, having served as the PR man for the Cubs during the Leo Durocher years. He was a man with a million stories, who had weathered the storm of the feisty "Leo the Lip" during faithful Cubs' fans most memorable and most painful season to date, the season of

98

1969. He had handled public relations, game promotions and ticket sales when the need came up. He was a baseball veteran man who didn't warm up to the millionaire players of today as much as he admired the blue-collar players of years past.

In addition to countless stories of the good old days, he could also name a million places he would rather be than stuck at the ballpark night after night. Under his gentle guidance, I developed a sense of flow for the game of baseball and, without even trying to be one, Charles Shriver became a great mentor to me and a dear, lifelong friend as well.

As I looked around Wrigley Field that day, nothing unusual happened to trigger my memories. They were just there, under the surface, neatly tucked away where I could retrieve them at a moment's notice. Good memories seem to make themselves available like that.

At that point in the year in early April, I was in the transition period where hockey would evolve into playoffs and then give way to baseball. That, coupled with the all day, every day, task of working on the startup of the Chicago Wolves Hockey Team was starting to weigh me down. I was tired and it was time for a break, but there was none in sight. No one, especially me, had any idea that the summer of 1994 would turn into what it did.

It was the beginning of my 13th season at the microphone of Major League Baseball. It was fairly routine to read through the copy, announce the hitters and, more often than not, sing the National Anthem to start things off. Yet, I still enjoyed the privilege of doing what I loved to do. As I chalked up another one for the record books, I realized that I was moving at a rate approaching the speed of light. I recognized that my workload was outpacing my available energy supply. My pride came in simply being a part of the rich and colorful history and tradition that lived within the Friendly Confines.

It was, and still is, amazing to me to recount some of the revered stories associated with the ballpark: the called shot of Babe Ruth in Game 3 of the 1932 World Series off Cubs' pitcher Charlie Root, the famous pinch-hit homer of player-manager Gabby Hartnett that sent the Cubs into the 1938 World Series with a win over the Pirates, the 500th Home Run of Mr. Cub Ernie Banks off of Atlanta's Pat Jarvis, the Bears' World Championship of 1963 when they defeated Y.A. Tittle and the New York Football Giants. It had been the scene of a seemingly endless list of sports moments.

I also fondly recall the rain-soaked night of August 8, 1988 or 8/8/88. Waiting in disappointment as the Cubs tried to celebrate their first-ever night game, only to be washed out just hours after octogenarian Cubs fan, Harry Grossman, flipped the symbolic switch and spoke his immortal words, "Let there be lights!"

It was the home of one of my fondest sports memories, a 1981 soccer match where the Chicago Sting defeated the New York Cosmos 5 to 4 in a shootout; a game that will give me chills even today when I recall it. I also laughed at the night game curse of the weather, as evidenced by the 1990 All-Star game when I sat for hours in the dugout, hoping for a chance to get to sing *O, Canada* and then introduce Richard Marx for the U.S. National Anthem following me. The wait was endless, but the time spent was well worth it as I enjoyed the moment and the lifelong memories I was given by just having been there.

The Cubs had been terrific to me. As the "Voice of Wrigley Field," I had been given the privilege of being exposed to millions of fans each day whenever I sang. With the expansive reach of WGN Television, the name of Wayne Messmer, and more specifically the voice, was pretty much a household word for Cubs fans from Bellingham, Washington to Belize. I wondered, "How could I ever consider walking away from that?"

The answer was that I couldn't. It had become too much a part of me. Over the years with the Cubs, I had shivered through the April and September months of hope and despair. I had baked in the dog days of summer heat and had seen my share of losses. Despite the countless hours spent in the unheated and unairconditioned PA booth, I would often find myself lost in the daze of contentment. During those moments, I admitted to myself that I frequently felt as though I had been born to do exactly what I was doing at that moment.

Representing the Cubs as their voice, speaking to the fans, was an awesome responsibility, one that I treated with the utmost respect and the dignity deserving of beautiful Wrigley Field. I recalled how I had developed a familiar and recognizable style and approach to the game over the years.

The legacy of Pat Pieper still lived within the hallowed ivy-covered walls. He'd spent just shy of 60 years, (1916-1974) as the Cubs field announcer and remained a colorful and historical personality, whom I held in great esteem. Pieper sat on the field for much of the time, using a megaphone to announce the batters. His career began during the age before a sound system was installed in the park.

Eventually, technology and probably a few too many foul balls and close calls forced the veteran upstairs to the old press box, which was replaced in 1990 when the luxury boxes were installed. There, the man who had worked Cubs' games by day and bussed tables at the nearby Ivanhoe Restaurant by night, was forced to view the game through failing eyes over his last few seasons.

Pieper grew irritated from his unfamiliar perspective and eventually gave way to Jim Enright, a retired sports writer who assumed the duties of the microphone. The legacy of being the man at the mic was a rich one. A position that needed to be carried out with pride. I was more than willing to be that guy. Pat Pieper's signature phrase invited people to pay attention as he gave the lineups.

"'Tention, 'Tention, please. Have your pencils and scorecards ready and I will give you the correct lineups for today's game. First, the batt'ry and the batting orders."

It was unique. The phrase was such a strong piece of the fiber of the Chicago National League Ballclub Incorporated that I wanted to keep it alive. I incorporated the words into my daily script. This was my daily or nightly greeting to the assembled masses as the show began.

"Good afternoon, ladies and gentlemen and welcome to Major League Baseball in the Friendly Confines of beautiful Wrigley Field, home of your Chicago Cubs."

Cheering would always happen.

"This is Wayne Messmer, speaking on behalf of the Cubs, welcoming you to today's game. The first of a three-game series between the visiting Los Angeles Dodgers and your Chicago Cubs."

That was always fun. The opening salvo was quickly followed by a flourish of chords played by organist Gary Pressy, one of the all-time die-hard Cubs fans and the man who filled the stadium with his music since he joined the club in 1987. It was an honor to be able to walk into the park, sit down at the microphone and transform myself into the voice of Wrigley Field for a few hours.

Through good games and bad, quick games and dragging extra inning affairs, rain delays and heat waves, spring chills and endless pitching changes, I was there from start to finish, or as I would point out, until I said "Thank you, drive safely." There were also more than a few times when I could actually feel the presence of history from the many lessons I had learned from watching the gentle game of baseball on a daily basis.

But in addition to looking into the past that day, I was also looking forward to a week away from the ballpark so I could devote some extra time to my latest business endeavor, the Chicago Wolves Hockey Team; a project requiring increasingly more of my time and attention. The schedule however, wasn't about to ease up. I was on tap to sing at Chicago Stadium both Friday night and Sunday afternoon, so the weekend offered no release. This was a typical example of what my schedule was like. It seemed that there was a full plate in front of me every single day.

The time demands of a long homestand often took their toll. Ten straight days at the park were followed by a welcomed break. I had hoped to get a breather. As it turned out, I got a much longer break than I could have possibly anticipated. My Wrigley Field memories were plentiful, but I now reflected with a sense of sadness that they now may be of a different nature. Standing on that historic field to start off a day of baseball was an honor I had never taken for granted. It was always a genuine thrill.

Now, as I stared down the path of a long, difficult period of recovery, I could sense being moved to tears with the thought that I might never have another opportunity to sing at Wrigley Field.

Sitting there in my room at Northwestern Memorial Hospital, I felt totally exhausted at the end of the day from hour after hour of intense emotions. I got a sense of just how big a news story my shooting was. I had been told about it, but it really hit home one afternoon when I saw the printed list of news reports from the media services detailing the coverage. I found the amount of media attention to be staggering.

Later that day, I discussed some important issues with the Wolves ad agency and a member of the Wolves Media Relations Department. They had been working to coordinate the news and information about my unfolding drama. We wanted to keep the flow of information consistent and accurate. Everyone was being careful not to release any statement on my condition unless we were absolutely sure of the facts.

Being cautious, I noticed that the stage was being set for the possibility of a not-so-spectacular finish to this tragedy that was being played out in front of my eyes and the eyes of everyone who was watching the TV and radio news or reading the daily accounts in the newspapers.

As I reviewed the news clippings of the past several days, my feelings ran from very interested, to cold, to fear and sadness. I was alright until I saw the one front page picture of my wife being comforted by one of my friends who had visited me earlier in the day. Suddenly, this was no longer a fantasy that someone was telling me in bits and pieces. This was a real live drama and I was the real person involved. For the first time, I could sense the enormous stress and anxiety this episode had placed on the rest of my family.

I made a pleasant discovery late in the afternoon that I had been breathing without distress since early morning. The tracheostomy tube had been downsized to a smaller size and had been capped. This meant that I was no longer requiring assistance from the tube in my throat just to breathe. I found myself once again looking forward to another exciting tomorrow. After a prayer of thanks for another day, it was time to sleep.

Wayne Messmer

The Voice Of Victory
Win One For Wayne

--The Chicago Sun-Times

"A journey of a thousand miles begins
with a single step"
--Chinese Proverb

Messmer 'Happy To Be Home' May Attend Attend Blackhawks Games

-- The Daily Herald

"We are what we repeatedly do.
Excellence then, is not an act, but a habit."
--*Aristotle*

Chapter 9

The Homecoming

Thursday, April 21, 1994

I spent a full day and night with the tracheostomy tube in my throat fully capped without any breathing difficulty. The prognosis from the doctors was very positive. A scheduled X-ray would check for nerve damage. Plans were to send a scope down my nose the next day. Hopefully the tube would be removed completely and then it was homeward bound.

Sitting in quiet reflection, I could not possibly ignore the overwhelming evidence of the power of prayer in my remarkable recovery, which was still a work-in-progress. I was being careful not to get caught up in my own press clippings, but I truly felt the way that Kathleen did; if anyone could do it, I could. In fact, I decided right then that I would.

Within the hour, I would have to recount the shooting incident in great detail for the record. This was to be my first opportunity to "speak" for myself about this tragic tale. I could only imagine the 15 and 16-year-old suspects in the case had no idea that this morning, when I gave my statement to the detective who made the arrests, that their fate would be officially sealed. Despite my eyewitness account of the crime, these young men provided the most damaging evidence against themselves two weeks ago when they had made some very poor choices in their lives.

I was feeling the full spectrum of emotions. Surprisingly, revenge was not one of them. I had come to realize that my attacker was a person who obviously had no concern for my life. I was continuing to search for a clue to help me understand how this young man could have tried to kill me without emotion, without as much as blinking an eye.

The second suspect in the shooting was being brought to Chicago from Louisville, Kentucky to face the charges. He was 16 years old. Upon hearing of his arrest and capture, I found that I was more saddened than excited by the news. I remember my own life at the age of 16. I recalled how I was just beginning to realize how great life was going to be. I was involved in music and thinking about the possibilities that were waiting for me. I did not recall ever feeling the urge to have a handgun and certainly never considered wanting to use one in an armed robbery.

Once again, I felt very grateful to my parents for providing a functional family with real Christian values with which I can live my life as an adult. I wondered where these boys' family structures and home environments had gone wrong.

I was troubled by the fact that while my two assailants may not have had the same opportunities in their lives or were not afforded the chance to know a healthy family environment as I did, these deficiencies would still not justify their actions. I was finding it difficult to accept any excuse for the cold-blooded attempt on my life.

Bit by bit, I heard the details of the 35 shootings that happened in Chicago on the same weekend when I was attacked. I found that number of shootings to be obscene. I consider myself to be one of the lucky ones; had survived.

As I thought about those other victims, Dr. Pelzer interrupted the silence when he called up to the room to verify the statement that he was about to make at a press conference outside of the hospital. Everyone was charged up with the story once again now that the FBI had arrested the second suspect. The big questions of the hour resurfaced: Will Wayne sing again? And: When is Wayne getting released?

Neither of those direct questions got a definitive response. I felt a bit of a chill as Dr. Pelzer told the media core that he's, "Not yet sure, and won't be for several weeks about the exact prognosis," of my speaking and singing voice. He also said that my day to day progress made him think I may be released next week. Dr. Pelzer held off the press with this optimistic, yet cautious, statement about my discharge from the hospital, although he and I both knew that the homecoming was imminent. I couldn't wait to go home.

Friday, April 22, 1994

This was to be my day. Show me the way to go home. Next stop: my own bed. Following the procedure to send a scope down my nose and check out the left side of my throat, we would hopefully have an accurate answer to the question of exactly how much damage was done when the 9mm slug ripped into my neck exactly two weeks earlier.

Dr. Pelzer went on TV again last night as the local newscast presented the story all over again. The big news hook was the arrest of the second suspect, but the issue continued to be the future of my singing career. That question could possibly be addressed by the scope within the hour.

I was anxious, but afraid of what the doctor might discover at the end of his lighted tube. Should he tell me that the left vocal cord was not damaged, it still could not assure me of a return to my music. The degree of the injury to my throat may have an impact on the voice in other ways, like pitch or intonation. Singing was still not an option in my immediate future, but I continued to recuperate and to hope.

110

I tried to sound out a note and discovered it to be more frightening than musical. I was disappointed, but not crushed. I had to try. I also had to tell myself, "It's still early." The good thing was that the tracheostomy tube was removed this morning. The two-week-old gash in my throat – one of several dramatic intervention steps that were taken to save my life – would eventually close up by itself, healing from the inside out. I took comfort in knowing that at least I would leave the hospital without a tube sticking out of my throat.

I also took notice of where I was in my journey of healing. Trying to remain positive, I focused on the future; where I was going and not so much on where I could have been.

After dressing myself at 6:00 a.m., I sat patiently and waited for the word that I could go home. Finally, Kathleen arrived and was surprised to see me so eager to leave. I proudly walked hand in hand with my beautiful wife, speaking words of thanks to the staff in a graveled voice as we exited Northwestern Memorial Hospital.

My sister, Barb, was with us as we stepped outside in the fresh late April air in the city that we loved so dearly. As we did, coincidentally, a friend was walking by just as we paused for a moment on the sidewalk before stepping into a waiting limo, which had been sent by the Chicago Cubs. He and I looked at each other and, without words, he spoke to me of the importance of the mission I would now face. Hiding behind the tears, his eyes were filled with love and hope.

It was the face of a man who had seen and heard me sing many times before. It was the heart of a man who refused to accept the possibility that he would never hear me sing again. Since that chance encounter, I've sung numerous times in this man's presence and neither of us will ever forget that brief, very private and highly symbolic moment of communication that we shared in one snapshot of time in our lives, without exchanging more than a few words.

The warmth of the spring sunshine was comforting, as was the realization that I had truly been blessed with an angel on both shoulders. God had touched my life. I knew that I could not forget the seriousness of the message that he had sent me. Yet, I continued to attempt to decipher exactly what that message might be.

Our daughter, Jennifer, came over to the house that afternoon to babysit for me. She had been so supportive throughout the whole ordeal. Our younger daughter, Stephanie, screamed with joy the night before, when I used what limited voice I had to speak with her by phone from her college room in Iowa City. She had been so frightened by the incident that I was pleased to be able to assure her that things would be calm again soon. Being away from home didn't help to ease her fear. I know that she desperately wanted to help. I let her know that her love was all that any of us truly needed.

I had seen our little family unit grow very close throughout this trying period in our lives. I am now able to better appreciate how a challenge can sometimes produce a stronger and even more solid bond of family unity among its members. Despite everything that had happened, my attitude remained consistent. I loved life with a passion. Even with the latest hand I'd been dealt, from my perspective, all things considered, it was still a pretty darn good hand.

Saturday, April 23, 1994

The newspaper headline read:

Messmer Happy to be Home; May attend Blackhawks Games

Nice thought, but untrue. I suppose I could have made a physical appearance at the games, just for the emotional factor. But the idea of being there without my voice was a bit too much for me. In my absence, Kathleen was a big hit at the Chicago Stadium again last night when she sang the National Anthem at a Chicago Bulls and Boston Celtics game. As part of the introduction, the PA announcer told the crowd that I had come home from the hospital earlier in the day. To which the crowd responded with a huge cheer.

It was another in a long list of flattering examples of the outpouring of love from my hometown of Chicago. I continued to marvel at the response from the fans.

My voice was still very rough and quiet, and my energy level would, without warning, drop away to near nothing. I think that the physical aspects of what had happened were finally starting to catch up with me. I wondered when the trauma and, possibly, the depression would ultimately kick in as well. I feared that it was coming, and if it did, I feared it would come crashing down on me.

I cooked breakfast and my sister, Barb, changed the dressing on my throat. The urge was to try to do too much too soon. I knew that and so did everyone else. The problem was that I was gaining a false sense of healing. Everything seemed to be fine other than the neck and throat injuries, which I realized must not be minimized. Physically, I was feeling just fine. It still would have been nice to have an idea about what damage had been done on the left side of my

113

throat. The speculation would continue until I could learn the cold, hard facts.

It was strange, but as each new day passed, singing was becoming less of a percentage of who I was. I kept repeating that if anyone could make a comeback from this, I could. I had developed a theory about why there was such an enormous reaction to the incident. People asked, "How could anyone shoot Wayne? He seems like a nice guy. How could anyone shoot the Voice of the National Anthem?" and the irony of it all, "How could they shoot him in the throat?"

I believed that many people reacted as if the National Anthem itself had been violated. Since I was the guy whom they had selected as their favorite person to sing it. I was still groping with the question of whether I would have been shot at all had I not tried to drive away from the danger scene or whether I would have been killed, had I not stepped on the gas pedal after getting hit. I realized that I would never know the answer to those questions. What I did know was that given the same circumstances, I would have had the same exact instinctive reaction, which was to get into the car and try to get to safety. The comfort of knowing that I did the right thing could not change the outcome of the incident, but at least it helped to ease my mind.

Sunday, April 24, 1994

For the first time in over two weeks, my name did not appear in a story in at least one of the daily newspapers. The dust was beginning to settle a bit, but the attention was still lingering. I was frustrated by the lack of volume I was able to produce with my voice and the obvious effort it took to produce any audible sounds at all. Patience had never been my strong suit, but I was growing increasingly anxious, despite the fact that I knew it would take some time to heal.

My energy level would still disappear at a moment's notice. A trip to one of my favorite breakfast places produced some comments and handshakes from the locals. I would guess that anyone who was marginally acquainted with the name Wayne Messmer, particularly in the Chicago area, was now aware of both the person and the story.

After breakfast, Kathleen and I went for a stroll in the forest preserve. We welcomed the chance to stand by a stream and listen to the sound of rushing water, providing us with another example of one of life's little pleasures. As we shared the moment, we acknowledged the fact that it was one of the many tender moments that we had reclaimed. Like all others, it too, had almost been lost to us.

Just down the block from our home, there was a park where kids played baseball and romped on the playlot. I couldn't resist the urge to walk down there just to see some happy young people playing. As I approached, I kept my distance so as not to be noticed. Sitting quietly in the outfield grass, I breathed in the smell of spring and enjoyed the sounds of laughter of the children. It was a good first step back to the world of beauty and goodness and away from the shadow of the oppressive cloud of tragedy and fear that had held us in its clutches.

As if it were planned, a thrown ball escaped the futile attempt of the young boy fitted with an oversized glove. It rolled right to me. As I picked it up and gently tossed it back, I wanted to say, "Thanks for letting me play." The experience was emotionally challenging. When my eyes started to well up with tears, I knew it was time to go home.

Little by little, I was beginning to find peace again in the world, in my life. And with each glorious breath I took, I increasingly thanked God for this second chance.

'Hawks' National Anthem Singer Recovering From Shooting

--The Indianapolis Star

"Do not try to be anything but what you are
-But try to be that perfectly."
--St Francis de Sales

2 Teens Held In Shooting Of Messmer

--*The Chicago Tribune*

"Forgiveness is the fragrance of the violet that clings to the heel that crushed it."
--Anonymous

Chapter 10
One Day, One Step At a Time

Monday, April 25, 1994

I felt that this was the first real day of my long-term recovery process. Now that the venue had shifted to home, the best I could do was wait. I suspected that the frustration would creep into the picture. Right after my injury, there was so much significant progress in such a short time. From this point on, small accomplishments would have to satisfy me.

My poor wife finally broke down and cried last night as we held each other. She had to be all things to all people during all of this from the beginning. I realized just how much I loved her. She was proving to be truly amazing.

The plans for the day were to rest and visit with my family. My parents came over after dropping off my sister Barb at the airport. She returned home to Albuquerque, NM after spending 10 days of nursing me back to health and good spirits. Once again, I feared that I may have failed to communicate to Barb just how much it meant to me to have her there with me every day. I always felt a great closeness with my big sister. Her patience and comfort had been a tremendous source of inspiration to me on many occasions. I only hoped that I was able to tell her just how much it all meant.

As for my voice, it was pretty much the same as the day before. There was still air escaping from the tracheostomy opening in my throat. It was distressing, but the wound would eventually heal in the next few days and my hopes were more intense than anyone's. I told Kathleen that I intended to come back all the way. She looked at me as if to say, "Tell me something I don't know." Her focus had been absolute and her conviction in the entire nightmare had been totally committed to full recovery.

With a partner like her and the continued prayer of thousands of friends and well-wishers, I must say I liked my chances. The frightening thing was that the doctors were still unable to successfully look down my throat to see what was going on inside the left side of my neck where I was shot. Internal swelling had blocked every previous attempt at getting a clear view of the damage, as well as the progress of the healing. This procedure would be attempted for the third time at Dr. Pelzer's office two days later. I was still very afraid of what they might find.

The peace and serenity of my neighborhood seemed to be calling me. With another cool spring day being given to us, it was a perfect setting to collect my thoughts. I did just that.

Tuesday, April 26, 1994

This was to be a very interesting late afternoon. Two gentlemen from the Cook County State's Attorney's Office came to the house to personally outline the details of the case against the two teens who had been arrested in connection with the crime. I had no idea what we would talk about or what they could possibly tell us about the case that we didn't already know. The anticipation was unnerving.

As I understood it, the cases against the young men were to be presented separately. I was comforted in the fact that it would be the State of Illinois versus the Defendants, not a "me versus them" scenario. I just hoped that the case or cases would be handled fairly.

I found myself getting enraged again. Anger seemed to be pouring out of me. I was upset over the loss of my voice and the pain that had been forced upon me. I was also confused by the lingering thoughts of my uncertainty about the future. I was starting to prepare and brace myself for whatever decision God would make for me in terms of my recovery. Yet I was still setting my sights on a full and complete return to my old form. I was trying to be careful not to fall into a fearful trap that appeared to be building in my subconscious. I was afraid that perhaps I was setting myself up for my life's greatest disappointment. I prayed that was not the case.

My friend who had been very supportive spoke to me about a rather sobering topic of long-term disability, loss of voice, in the event that my physical comeback might stop short of the completion that I had in mind. It made me realize that not everyone was taking my recovery for granted. I admitted to myself that it was probably healthy to hear a realistic voice from the other side of the fence.

I seemed to be gaining energy. I was able to stay charged from about 7:00 am until 1:00 p.m.. Six entire hours. It was still not enough of a battery charge to completely jump back in the saddle, but it was a dramatic improvement over the past few days since I had been home.

Another dear friend made a wonderful suggestion today. Sensing firsthand my frustration at the slow response I was having with my voice, he told me to read a paragraph or two from the newspaper aloud each day and to record it. I liked the idea. At least this way I would be able to rewind and keep a log of the vocal progress and to maybe be able to hear some improvements after a while. I desperately wanted to make it work. I soon positively discovered that it did.

I likened the suggestion to one you might offer a dieter who weighed himself or herself every day. The small amount of progress would be so hard to detect from one day to the next. It will be easy to give up. I imagine this as another hurdle to clear. Even though it might be tough to stick with, I knew I was up to the challenge.

I found that I was constantly being motivated by the positive attitude of my wife, whose daily doses of encouragement were the exact prescription I needed to keep my chin up and to focus on our collective goal of simply getting better. From her, I was learning the painful lesson of patience.

Wednesday, April 27, 1994

Another attempt at getting a look at the internal damage on the left side of my throat ended as another inconclusive trip down my nose. Despite the fact that three weeks had passed, the swelling inside my throat continued to hamper the successful completion of examination. Even with the latest disappointment, Dr. Pelzer was not the bearer of bad news. Yet, he wasn't able to be terribly encouraging either.

He began to prepare me in a rather subtle fashion for some possible bad news down the road. He talked about some options in the event that the left vocal cord did not respond. I learned of the work of a surgeon in Cleveland, OH, who was known to be successfully performing a procedure whereby he would replace a damaged or paralyzed vocal cord with another muscle or tissue. However, we still had to consider the possibility that my nerves were damaged. Should this be the case, it would be devastating news for me. It would mean permanent vocal paralysis on the left side of my throat. The visit left me rather depressed, but still not defeated.

Once again, it was time to deal with the options. I was facing the unwelcome, yet realistic possibility of a life without singing. I kept trying to force myself to adjust to a slow and steady recovery. At the same time, I was also trying to convince myself to be cautious and to not accept lofty expectations that other people had for me.

A number of concerned folks continued to call. It was very encouraging to hear about the prayers and see the cards continue to come in from all over the country. I was pleased to read a very warm note from the Illinois Governor Jim Edgar and his wife, Brenda as well as a personal handwritten note from First Lady, Hillary Rodham Clinton.

Again, I tried some vocalization with unhappy results. My frustration level reached its peak at a morning meeting with a speech therapist earlier in the day as she attempted to put me through some exercises. The damage became more apparent when I tried and failed in an attempt to do the simplest vocalizing without success. "Remember the lesson in patience you learned yesterday," I told myself.

Thursday, April 28, 1994

"I feel better now that I've seen you." That seemed to be the comment of most people after a visit. What was it that folks expected when they saw me? I was not really sure. Perhaps the fact that I was up and walking, breathing without assistance and communicating with a semi-recognizable voice was enough to perk up the spirits of the family and friends who came over to the house to take a look.

I awoke early with a frightening anxiety attack. In my mind, I was replaying the songs I sang to my beautiful wife just a few months ago at our 10th anniversary when we renewed our wedding vows. I adamantly refused to accept the glaring signals that the sentimental and romantic musical moments we had shared that evening were lost forever. "Forget the National Anthem. Don't even think about musical theater," I told myself. "My biggest musical loss would be that that duo of Wayne and Kathleen Messmer, 'sophisticated musical entertainment,' as we were billed, were now silenced." I would simply, not allow anyone to steal that privileged bond that we had together.

Emotions were running very high that morning and I feared a meltdown coming on. It would be so easy to pull away from the world and hide inside a shell. I could not allow myself to do that. Although the temptation was extremely strong. The thought was to keep the marketing phrase of the final season of Chicago Stadium alive, and "Remember the Roar!" I used those words as a rallying cry to keep pushing forward. When do I speak publicly? To whom? And more importantly, what do I say?

These were the questions I needed to address soon. Finding some comfort in tranquility, I welcomed the time to heal the body and, certainly, the mind. These were still the most vital needs I had in my life. My source of strength continued to emerge from Kathleen's courage. My amazing wife refused to waiver in the quest for my recovery. "Somehow," I told myself, "I will use whatever remaining talents I have to satisfy my need to perform musically with my partner in life." This was a promise.

The next step remained a mystery. I felt as though I was standing on a diving board thinking about which difficult dive I would choose to attempt. I knew there were a number of options with varying degrees of difficulty, but I wanted to make sure that I made the right choice. I reaffirmed my commitment to put my recovery in the hands of God. Whatever choice He made for my future, I would accept.

Friday, April 29, 1994

The most inspiring note I received in several days arrived on this day in the mail. It was a priceless handwritten message from my sweet daughter, Jennifer. It read:

Watching you lie in a hospital bed has taken me through the most emotional time of my life. I saw the fear, anger and love in your expressions every day. I may not tell or show you enough how you have made me into the person I am today. You and Mom have taught me trust and respect and have shown me how to love.

You are a father who gives me advice and my very dear friend who shows me the joys of life. The friendship that we have developed can never be replaced. As the days ahead may bring a lot of battles, I want you to remember that you are a part of a very special family who loves you very much.

Love,

Jen

I would never forget this note. It would be a part of my life from that day forward. "It's a great day to be alive," I said with a smile.

Saturday, April 30, 1994

I continued to brace myself for what could be, not what everyone else assumed would be. My attitude remained focused, yet I was the only one who could feel the strains of the healing in the interior of my throat and in the obviously reduced airway passage. Singing was still light years away, but my speaking voice was probably 35 to 40 percent of what it used to be. I was finding confidence in the increased volume of the voice based on my own therapy of breathing and vocal exercises.

I had to admit that I was not as frustrated with my speaking voice at this point as I expected that I might be. Three weeks ago, I was lying unconscious in intensive care with friends and family hovering over me, fearing the worst. I had made great strides in terms of physical recovery in a short time. While I recognized that the road ahead was still lengthy, I was encouraged by the fact that I was showing signs of improvement every day.

I got a surprise call at the house when former Cubs great Andy Pafko phoned just to say hello and see how I was doing. The sheer numbers of people who stepped forward was very humbling. I realized that, like most people who have been incapacitated, I was not only aware of who had expressed their concerns, I could not help but notice the absence of contact from others.

Father David Ryan, who was the Assistant Executive Director at a remarkable life-changing facility in the Chicago area, which houses troubled and abused children, called me to send his good wishes. He had been one of the first people to come to the aid of my family within hours after the news of the shooting was announced. He led the boys in prayer at Mass over the past three weeks.

The amazing thing was that these kids under his watch had come from broken and abusive homes. In many cases, considerably worse than the home environments of the two young men who attacked me. Yet, they were being taught the values to have a concern with the welfare of others. I knew that the work being done at Maryville was truly inspirational. I considered Fathers Ryan and John Smyth, Maryville's executive director, to be living examples of God's work being done in our midst. I also consider their friendship to be near the top of the list of my life's greatest gifts.

Father John Smyth was a legendary figure. He passed on an opportunity to play professional basketball following a spectacular collegiate career at Notre Dame in order to enter the priesthood. His ministry has saved the lives of countless thousands of young men over the course of his tenure. It was his words, spoken in a simple sermon one Sunday morning in the Maryville Chapel that first led me to the understanding and appreciation of the powerful foundation of the "3-F's" – of Faith, Family and Friends. The trilogy had become my personal source of strength over the period of recovery and rehabilitation and has since been adopted as my personal philosophy, along with the fourth and fifth F's of Forgiveness and Freedom.

I continued to be eternally grateful to those two men of God. I returned their favor with several prayers of my own for the continuation of their important work.

Strike Affords Messmer A Chance For Final Tuneup

--The Chicago Tribune

"Destiny is not a matter of choice; it is not a thing to be waited for, it is a thing to be achieved."
--William Jennings Bryan

Messmer Recovering

-- The Peoria Journal-Star

"Music expresses that which cannot be put into words and that which cannot remain silent."
--Victor Hugo

Chapter 11

I'm Beginning To See The Light

Sunday, May 1, 1994

I was elated to turn the calendar over and put April 1994 into the history books. It ended with an emotional outburst late in the last night of the month as, once more, I questioned the reason this whole thing happened. Naturally, I was willing to blame myself for being in the wrong place at the wrong time. The second-guessing was enough to put me in a quivering state of tears. Only the comforting hugs from my beautiful wife helped to pick up the pieces.

Kathleen held me tight and let it all pour out without judging, without guilt, without fear. I came to realize more and more every day what impressive strength my partner had for both of us.

To start the month of May, we attended morning Mass at St. Emily's Catholic Church, our nearby parish. The experience was positive; good music, meaningful readings and a well-delivered sermon. My dear wife started to cry once again during the closing hymn, which called for the congregation to sing to the mountains... "for this is the day the Lord hath made," from Psalm 118. I would have loved to have been able to sing to the mountains, but at that point I would have gladly settled for the opportunity to just see them and quietly speak about their splendor. The song would come soon enough.

My faith and trust in God continued to grow stronger each day. While in church, I repeated my prayer to place the fate of my healing in His hands. I vowed that I would accept, without descension, whatever decision God made for me in this draining experience.

I spoke with my sister-in-law, Joan, who offered some needed support in a phone conversation. She and Kathleen's brother, Jack, who is an Episcopalian priest, led a large prayer group on my behalf at Jack's parish in Seattle. Joan was pleased to hear what voice I had and was equally pleased to hear that I had come to the tranquil point of placing my fate in the hands of God. We spoke of what message I might be able to transmit through my recovery, regardless of the final results. We both know that my work was far from over and her spirit and Jack's faith were very comforting to me.

Ironically, a feature on Dennis Byrd, a former pro-football player, was on TV that night. He talked about the miracle of recovery from his devastating football injury that left him on the brink of paralysis. He too had to reach deep inside himself for the strength to survive. He simply refused to accept defeat. That was the only attitude that would work in challenging times such as these. I echoed his strength and resolve, but also admitted that I did so with caution, should my vocal instrument be damaged beyond repair, which was still unknown, nothing would bring it back. At the risk of sounding pessimistic, I was just trying to prepare to not be completely devastated should the truth end up being something less than what I was hoping and praying for.

I continually called to mind the words of Jesus, who left us with the command, "Go and spread the word." I prayed that he would recognize the fact that I needed a voice to speak this message and sing His praises. I had a good feeling that He was listening to my plea.

As the church service concluded, in my heart I was singing out in full voice. "This is the day the Lord hath made. Rejoice and be glad in it." I am so very happy to be alive.

Monday, May 2, 1994

I was mobile again. The infamous car, which everyone in the city saw on TV at the scene of the crime, was now back in my possession. The shattered window had been replaced, thanks to my dad. Somehow, getting into the car and driving it that morning was not as eerie as I had initially feared it might be. Life had to go on and I needed to get around. That was all there was to it.

Kathleen, who seemed to be there at every crucial moment, again subdued a 3:00 a.m. panic attack. I found myself having difficulty breathing; feeling as though I were choking. The helplessness of not being able to catch my breath was enough to put me into a state of frightened anxiety.

After several minutes of slow, deep breaths and some comforting words from my partner, I was able to calm down and eventually fall asleep again. Another crisis, and another crisis conquered by Kathleen.

I remembered a time a few years before when it was my wife who was sick following complications from gallbladder surgery. At that time, I bought some roses and a card for her to welcome her back to life when she finally came home after a month of hospitalization. My sweetheart did the same thing for me this day. Roses and a card celebrating life and our love sat on the piano in our living room as a symbol of progress and hope for the future and our lives together.

I felt that it would soon be time that I made a statement to the media. A veteran Chicago newsman called me and offered himself as a potential outlet for an exclusive interview. He wanted to talk with me in my car at the scene of the shooting. "Great for his ratings," I thought, "but bad for my psyche." In spite of his repeated phone calls, I declined the request. I wanted to think about with whom I would sit to tell my story if I decided to tell it at all. My initial comments, I thought, had to be carefully chosen.

Speaking on the issues of faith, life, family and street violence, I felt I could make an impact by saying thank you for the thousands of cards I received from fans, Chicagoans and the crowds of people from all 50 states and as far away as Europe. These were individuals with whom I had never had personal contact or had never met. Obviously, they too were appalled by this senseless and still unexplainable act.

I refused to feel sorry for myself. This was a trap into which I was careful not to fall. Why me? Why in the throat? Despite my caution, these questions kept haunting me. They were difficult to ignore, no matter how positive I forced myself to remain.

Our little dog, "Squirt," came home after staying with my parents for three weeks. It was nice to see my little pal back in our home. She could sense that something was wrong, but she was not quite sure what it was or how she could help. As loyal pets have a way of comforting often much more effectively than humans, she did just the right thing by just being a friend. That was already a big help.

Tuesday, May 3, 1994.

It was National Teacher Appreciation Day. I announced my appreciation for Kathleen when she came home from her day of instructions with her first graders. My superheroes are teachers for what they do and the role they play in the lives of children. She is certainly one of the best in the business.

During the early morning, I sat there with the entire student body of St. Emily's School during Mass. The children were there to participate in the ceremony and to celebrate Teacher Appreciation Day. It was an experience that caused me to stop and think about the children of the world and how I might relate to them with my message when I started sharing it. I decided that my story would focus on family values and the importance of responsible parenting and not on the popular topic of gun control.

My message had to be heard so that people would come to understand and accept their own responsibilities as they relate to the actions and behavior of their children. The thought of a 15-year-old walking the streets at 1:30 a.m. with a loaded handgun, waiting for the next victim to come by was a perfect example of the results of a breakdown of the traditional two-parent family structure. I felt the overwhelming need to speak out with emotion and conviction to underscore the importance of gaining control of our streets and rebuilding the infrastructure of our families.

I knew that this message now surfacing in my mind was extremely important. I also knew there was some work to do as I continued to deal with my anger and leftover second-guessing. But I was also making a solid plan for recovery for my life as a survivor, not as a victim.

A number of phone calls helped me to see that the time was drawing near to step forward and make a public statement of some substance. If not now, then I was aware that my career path – wherever it would eventually take me – would be filled with opportunities to speak out on these important issues that had become so important to me.

My physical strength was also returning. I would soon be able to stand at attention and say to the world, "I am a survivor. I am here as a tribute to the strength of my faith, family and friends and the enormous power of prayer." I was anxious for that day to arrive.

Kathleen filled in for me at yet another singing appearance. She sang in my place at the Illinois Safety Council Annual Meeting. I had appeared before the group as soloist myself for a number of years before this night. My dear friend, who was the president of the group, had invited her. She sang beautifully and read a short message to the attendees who received her with open arms. Chalk up another gold star for the best partner in the world and a terrific singer to boot.

As she sang in the ballroom of the hotel, I waited quietly in the lobby where I stepped into the light just long enough to have a brief embrace from my friend who had stepped out of the meeting to greet me upon Kathleen's invitation. I enjoyed visiting with a friend, but I knew I was still not quite ready to face the world, despite my rising confidence. "Soon," I told myself.

Wednesday, May 4, 1994

Tonight would be a major test of strength of my positive attitude. Kathleen and I had planned to attend a professional theatrical production of a musical named *Windy City*. We had been going to shows at this particular theater for several years as season ticket holders and I always related very personally to the singing on stage. Being in an arena of musical theater where I had enjoyed so many wonderful moments in the past turned out to not be as uncomfortable as I had feared. I found that watching and listening to the actors actually gave me encouragement to work harder. The power of positive thinking was paying a dividend.

Instead of leaving the theater depressed, I was ready to continue my work – although the loss of my singing voice, permanently or even just temporarily, weighed heavily on my mind. I forced myself to focus on the future and recognize that it possibly may not return. I also discovered that while I may not be ready to go back on the stage, I was still a pretty good audience member. "Appreciate the little victories one at a time," I told myself. I had made it this far.

Friday, May 6, 1994

I wanted to hold a press conference next week, but it would have been delayed for the week of May 16 when Dr. Pelzer would be available. He had been a key player in the picture, so I was very willing to accommodate my schedule around his. In our last conversation, he delivered some good news and some non-news. After reviewing a CT scan that I had taken the previous day, he advised me that the arytenoid cartilage seemed to be in good shape, although there was some displaced thyroid cartilage. That, coupled with some residual swelling and the lingering hematoma, gave me a complete a picture as possible. I only wish that I had paid attention a little closer to the medical shows on TV, so I might have possibly understood what he had just told me. I also wished that I had written something down.

There was still no explanation for the reason behind the inactivity of my left vocal cord. The possibility of nerve damage was still very real. A rather bizarre set of tests where needles would be inserted directly into my throat would be required to determine the extent of the damage, should some damage actually be present. I did not look forward to any of that.

Among the list of people who called me to assess my condition was a dear man named Al Goldis, the Cubs VP of Player Development at the time. Al was a very kind and intelligent man who had spent time as a teacher, a New York cab driver and a clothing designer in addition to his recognized abilities to evaluate baseball talent. He remained a good friend since we had first met professionally two years previous. His sense of humor came at a most welcomed moment.

It was the simple acts of kindness which seemed to stick in my mind. This morning, I cleared my very important hurdle when I went to Parkview School to read a book for Kathleen's first graders. I had been there earlier in the school year with full voice. I needed to retrace the steps for my own confidence.

I read a book entitled, *A Duck Named Ping*. The children sat quietly, listening to me read without complaining that I couldn't be heard or understood. I left the classroom with a major boost in my confidence level as I continued my recovery. Again, I was impressed by the power of children to deliver a message of hope and acceptance just through their innocence, without speaking a word. It felt wonderful and I let them know it.

Our schedule for the evening called for us to see a performance of another musical. This time it would be familiar actors with whom we had worked in the past. These were many of the same people we both knew and with whom we had stood on stage in numerous performances. Before the incident, I had been asked to audition for this very show, where the connection was quite personal. I was curious to see the reaction of the other actors when we all saw each other. People are always uncomfortable in such situations; not knowing what to say, so they often say nothing. I promised myself to keep the first graders' smiling and

137

contented faces in my mind as I met the well-wishers of the theater that evening.

I learned another of life's important lessons that night. The actors were more than just people on stage. They were my friends. Each of them in their own way expressed a vote of confidence that I would regain the gift of my voice. Each one also told me how they valued my friendship over everything else. I was humbled and once again very grateful. It had been a most incredible day.

Sunday, May 8, 1994

It was Mother's Day and the gift for which my Mom would be most pleased was the fact that her youngest son was alive. I think that we all appreciated the significance of this gift. At church that morning, I attempted to bellow out a few strains of the hymns in a low octave, managing to get a smile out of my bride for the latest vocal attempt. It seemed obvious that my voice was probably going to be different. I had come to recognize that already. Just how different it would be was a mystery. It was still very premature, but the nagging feeling in the back of my mind was telling me that the damage would probably prohibit my full recovery.

This was the point of recovery where the injured person actually becomes their own worst enemy. I fought the urge to give in to the temptation to accept defeat.

I was now quietly and very privately preparing myself for less than complete recovery, although I did not dare to share this with Kathleen. I was starting to have serious doubts. I felt that I was being realistic. Despite my personal feelings about the prognosis, I continued to try and vocalize something new each day. Maybe it was a children's tune, a familiar phrase from a show or a line or two from the National Anthem. Every day, a little test.

When I opened my mouth and the voice didn't work – and it usually didn't – I would try another tune. "Too many songs to get hung up on just one," I told myself, laughing as I recalled the number of times I had been asked if I knew any other song besides the National Anthem.

I made plans to enjoy a peaceful day at home with my parents to spend time with us, along with Kathleen's mother, whom we affectionately called by her initials, E.T. Her name was Elaine Tench. Our daughter, Jennifer, would also be there. She would always add a lot to any gathering.

My role was to be the BBQ chef and happy host. Things had come a long way in the one month since the shot heard around the City of Chicago had changed our lives.

Kentucky Teen Faces Charges Related To Messmer Shooting

--The Daily Herald

"The glory of Christianity is to conquer by forgiveness."
--William Blake

Wayne-Derful Moment

--*The Chicago Sun-Times*

"The best Anthem singer I ever heard in 21 years in the NHL."
--Hockey Hall of Famer Stan Mikita

Chapter 12
What's Up, Doc?

Monday, May 9, 1994

I had been thinking a lot about what punishment I felt should be or would be handed out to the pair of individuals involved in my attack. This was actually a moot point since I had long since come to the realization that justice was not mine to distribute. I found myself in a confusing and powerless position. More and more, people were willing to offer their opinion that I should simply be glad that I was alive and not be so concerned with the possibility of regaining full use of the speaking and singing voice.

The advice was not always accepted as welcome words of encouragement. Instead, I began to get irritated when I heard people offering their opinions that I should settle for less. In many ways, I was afraid that people were picking up on my inner fears.

No one but Kathleen and I could appreciate the important part of me that was now missing. Sure, it had only been a month and I understood that the damage was severe and the trauma substantial. Yet, I would have liked to have had an idea whether I had sung my last tune. I was becoming impatient with the act of trying to be patient. The needle test for the possibility of nerve damage had still not taken place. Meanwhile, my left vocal cord remained paralyzed and virtually useless. I was working every day on trying to discover a comfortable technique for producing at least the beginning of some vocal, if not musical, sounds. It used to come so easily and effortlessly.

Now, each note I attempted presented a major challenge. I still suspected that the quality of my singing voice would be drastically altered, yet I felt willing to make my comeback possibly with a new sound. I tried to recall stories of other singers who had salvaged their careers by overcoming serious vocal injuries. I planned to add my name to that list of those who had met the challenge head-on and had overcome adversity with hard work.

I sprinkled my throat with holy water from the holy shrine at Lourdes, France as part of my morning ritual of prayer. I was placing an even more intense emphasis on faith as my physical progress continued to move very tediously.

Sorting through the memories of the beautiful day we had spent with the family on Sunday, I was delighted by the fact that my Mom had been with me on Mother's Day. Even more significantly, I was enormously thankful to be alive and to have spent the day with her.

Throughout my life, I had always felt that God had heard her prayers and devotions. I considered this special day to be an answered prayer. I recall that it had been a good day for all of us. One in a series of many we hoped to enjoy as a family.

Tuesday, May 10, 1994

Seriously considering my probable limitations, I continued to wonder where I would go and what I would do throughout the next few weeks and months to make the next several years worthwhile. I was convinced that the important thing was to move ahead with the next step in my career, whatever that may turn out to be. The cloud of uncertainty would not allow me to make such a crucial life-changing decision quite yet.

I found myself looking back to evaluate my life before the injury. I considered how the priorities had shifted. Things had drastically changed already. My options had also been changed as a result of the limitations that I was now facing. I couldn't help but think that the healing process would bring me to the point where I was able to continue my working routine. My question was whether or not I wanted to resume where I had left off, should I be afforded that opportunity.

There were a lot of items of which I had to take inventory during that period of disability. I considered and reconsidered my priorities. These were hard lessons to face and even harder lessons to accept. I thought about the very personal relationships which I had cultivated over the years with the Chicago Cubs, the same team now flying a WM flag over Wrigley Field, awaiting my return to the PA Announcer's booth. I thought about the friendships I had developed with the members of the team's marketing department. I didn't want to let them down. They had been so supportive in my professional and now my personal life. I flashed back on the list of other important relationships I had developed over the years and fondly remembered how they had made a lasting mark on my mind.

I was simply not willing to let it all go. The lifelong bond that I had made with the Cubs and the thousands of loyal Cubs' fans had grown to be very precious to me. Soon, I knew I would have to consider the next step in the continuing saga of "The Guy Who Sings the Anthem." My options were being weighed in terms of the healing process. It was now a matter of what I could do, not what I wanted to do.

That was a major departure of how my professional career had evolved since I first started making a living with my voice. I felt the need to return to Wrigley Field as the PA

Announcer to be both a personal as well as a psychological victory. Then, if God allowed, I would also want to return as the National Anthem singer as well. Only time would tell.

Speaking again with the Cubs, I discovered a genuine and sincere concern for my well-being. They were not only looking at my physical healing, but they also recognized the inner turmoil with which I was wrestling. I was assured that my job as the Cubs PA Announcer would be waiting for me, no matter how long it took. I was also told that I shouldn't feel that I needed to wait until I could deliver the whole package of announcing and singing the Anthem again before planning a return to the ballpark. I was assured the Cubs would welcome me home in either capacity or both.

I appreciated the confidence, but I was fighting the mounting fear that regardless of how hard I tried, the voice might never be well enough to allow me to make those choices. I tried to hide my fears from the rest of the world, but I couldn't help them from eating me alive.

In my daily pep talk to myself, I recognized how personally important it was for me and for my mental health to return to the point of walking back into Wrigley Field to resume my life. This vision had become an obsession. I repeated the thought again and again, but still had a difficult time convincing myself that it would really happen one day.

Wednesday, May 11, 1994

As I pulled up to Northwestern Memorial Hospital, I was gripped with fear and anxiety. This would finally be the day when I would find out once and for all just how bad the damage to my throat actually was. I would also find out if the damage was permanent.

After repeated failings and previous exams, I was determined to get an answer one way or the other. The doubting and the unanswered questions had gone on far too long. This was to be the moment of truth. To me, this had all the indications of being the major turning point. The results of this exam contained the answer to the burning question that had tormented me since I first opened my eyes a month ago. Obviously, I knew there was damage. The questions that haunted me were: How much? How bad? How permanent? I had to trust that by the time I left the examining table, I would have the information I needed to set the course for the rest of my life. The pressure was intense.

After a short time in the waiting room, I was brought in to the examination room and told to lay down on the table. The doctor began to insert long needles into my throat in a manner resembling acupuncture. I had to remain perfectly still so that he could get a reading of the nerve activity in the damaged area of my neck. I resisted the urge to cough. I had been told that the slightest movement could force him to have to start the test all over again. I was motionless, almost holding my breath. "Once is enough," I told myself, picturing the image of my profile as a porcupine with several needles now protruding from my neck.

The doctor left the examining room to read the probes. As he exited the room, I felt more alone than I have ever at any point before in my life. It seemed like hours before he came back, although it was probably no more than 10 minutes. When he did return, it was only to reinsert one of the larger metal needles into my neck. Safe to say that I was not having fun.

Finally, the door opened, and he stood before me, expressionless. He indicated no hint of whether he was about to deliver good news or bad. "The test looks good," he said, without providing any details of his scientific probing. And...

"What exactly does that mean?" I asked. "Does this mean there is no nerve damage?" I held my breath and he paused to answer the most important question of my recent life. "That's right. I don't see any permanent damage to the nerves."

I felt the compulsion to probe him right back. "Does this mean that in time the vocal cords might resume their normal function?" I snapped back. "I don't see why not," he said, with a cold, almost matter-of-fact look. I almost jumped off the table. Here, I had just been given the green light to a complete recovery and the doctor who delivered the news acted as if he were no more enthused than if he were reading a thermometer.

I quickly realized that the news was certainly more significant to me than it was to the doctor, who viewed me as just another patient in an endless parade to come into his examination room. "Bedside manner be damned," I said to myself. I was now the bearer of great news. Half-voice or not, I was going to shout as best I could to the world, "Watch out! I'm unstoppable now."

As I left the hospital, I paused in the chapel to say just two powerful words that were abundant in gratitude, "Thank you," I said. From that moment, I knew that I had been given the gift a second time. Although I recognized that this time there would have to be some assembly required.

Calling Kathleen to tell her the news was one of the most joy-filled moments that I have ever experienced. "We're going to do it!," I told her with all of the enthusiasm that I could muster. "Of course we are," she said, confidently. She had never stopped believing in me and in us, and had never doubted her faith for even a second.

Wayne Messmer

Messmer Visits Wrigley, Vows To Sing Again

--The Chicago Sun Times

"Don't wait for your ship to come in, swim out to it."
--Anonymous

148

Wayne's World Messmer Throws Out First Pitch

--The Chicago Sun-Times

"Wayne is the Cubs' answer to Caruso,
Hey! Hey!
--HOF Broadcaster Jack Brickhouse

Chapter 13

Facing The Challenge Of Change

The time had now arrived to put the foundation of my beliefs and my philosophy of life to the test. Hard work and plenty of it were the order of the day. I retraced my steps once again, thinking of how I had been on a constant roller coaster of emotions since the moment I had been injured. Once again, I was taken back to the moment of truth, those critical minutes that had been permanently imprinted in my memory.

In the immediate moments after the attack, as I lay there, I knew that all I had worked for may have been stolen from me. As I sat waiting for medical assistance, one of the first thoughts that entered my mind was that my life was changing before my eyes. It was obvious that the instrument of my voice had been damaged – so much so that I feared it may have already been rendered useless. I had no way of knowing that, yet I still had the thought on my mind, "What do I do now?"

I began to run through the files that I had accumulated in my mind; files of information and inspiring quotes that I hoped were real now that I needed to hear them. More importantly, I needed to be able to believe them, not just remember the words.

The challenge of change was a topic that I had spoken to various groups about many times. This challenge was now staring me directly in the eyes. How I responded to it was the key to my future. I had found that the choice of words can be very powerful or very crippling. Instead of seeing my

150

situation as a challenge of change, I chose to use the phrase "opportunity for improvement." I knew the shooting had put me in the spot and would be a sobering test that would challenge my innermost beliefs. Time and again, I had stood before groups as their keynote speaker and talked about how we are often our biggest obstacle to our own growth. We are responsible for setting our own traps, by being unprepared for change when it ultimately arrives, and, despite our protestations, change is always just around the corner.

Like most people, I try to stay ahead of the times by keeping abreast of the trends and listening to the latest ideas. Still, when your world comes to an abrupt halt, the feeling of helplessness can be all-consuming. Most people, when their existence hits a major speedbump, want to ask, "Why me?" This is a classic victim statement of entrapment. I refused to be obsessed with the question.

I believe that everything happens for a reason. What was the reason? The fact is that I didn't know then and I'm not sure that I know now. I only know this: in order to heal and turn our disasters to our advantage, we need to stop asking, "Why me?" and start asking, "Why not me?" To be a card-carrying member of the human race requires that we pay some dues to enjoy the privileges. Last time I checked, no one gets out of this game alive. Everything carries a price.

In my case, I felt that God was not ready to put me to work in his Kingdom yet. That was the only explanation I was willing to acknowledge for why my life had been spared that night.

Change has a way of sneaking up on you. Just like old age. The best laid plans are often swept right out from under us just when we least expect it. I love the phrase asking, "If you want to make God laugh? Tell Him your plan."

I became acutely aware of what it means to place your trust in a higher being. I had to trust. My bearings had been shaken to the point where everything I had come to accept as truth had been put to the test. But I recognized immediately that even though the attack may change my career, it would not alter who I was. This almost immediately helped to put me on the right track psychologically. Knowing yourself is the best information you can carry with you.

About ten days after my attack, I had built up the courage and the strength to take my first look in the mirror to assess the damage. I looked beyond the bandages and the wounds and looked deeper into the person standing there. The moment of absolute honesty can either inspire you to go forward or stop you dead in your tracks. I chose the former, as well as life, and have never turned back since.

My life had revolved around the use of my voice for so many years, so the sight was staggering. I recall slowly removing the bandages covering my throat to reveal the aftermath of the lifesaving surgery. It was a frightening sight in that mirror. A living, breathing portrait in reflective glass that represented a snapshot in time in this confusing chapter of my existence. Was this the opening frame or was it the final one? It was a question I had to ask, but for which I didn't want an answer. Not then. It was still too soon.

The first glance took my breath away. The incision spanned the distance from ear to ear, interrupted only by the intrusive tracheostomy tube that was still quite necessary in order to breathe. I pictured myself on the operating table, looking like a Pez© dispenser when they were in mid-surgery. The chuckle I got from the image came at just the right moment.

Countless times in my motivational speaking appearances, I had used the phrase, "The mirror doesn't lie.

It speaks to us even when we would rather not hear it and the words are few but poignant." It says in a voice sounding very much like our own, "You're not fooling me." I knew I had a lot of work to do. That mirror spoke in a voice with a familiar tone that had provided a career in radio, speaking and singing for nearly two decades already and I would not allow it to be stolen. It was a voice that, at that point, I recognized only as a memory.

After that first look in the mirror, I sat quietly and peacefully. The words of the Lord's Prayer was especially meaningful as I sought comfort and guidance. *Thy will be done.* This was my moment of truth. This was where faith, belief and trust must come together in a moment of epiphany when all you have ever recognized and accepted to be your faith clearly presents itself before your eyes. This moment opened my eyes to a new line of communication in my prayer life, one that I hoped would help me to accept my fate.

I found the strength to make the decision to not accept the label of victim in this situation. Instead, I consciously took on the title of victor. I learned that the psychological line between these states could indeed be very thin, but most significant.

It became obvious to me that while my setback was physically devastating at the moment, feeling sorry for myself would have no immediate or long-range impact on my recovery. The "poor me" mentality is tremendously crippling. "It entraps you in the role of the victim. Where you need to be cast is in the role of survivor," I firmly said to myself silently over and over again.

After the incident, I had plenty of quiet time to pray and reflect on life. My challenges were; to stay alive, to speak again and, if at all possible, to sing again. This clear and narrow focus put me on the path to not only getting well, but also being better. I hoped that the lessons I would learn would give me a greater sense of understanding and acceptance of others who had traveled the same journey, or would do so in the future.

I knew the odds were against me physically, but no one was able to examine the desire in my mind and in my heart. That was not recorded on any chart. My spiritual and emotional health was up to me during the recovery process. I realized that I would be as spiritually and emotionally healthy as I decided to be.

Fortunately for me, both of these critical areas of my being were not injured, nor had they been suffering before the shooting. This distinction helped me to recognize that I had been living the message of readiness when, not if, a crisis would enter my otherwise well-charted life. I decided that my story was going to have a happy ending. The only way I could see it was to take authorship of my own life's script. Taking the figurative pen in hand, I began charting the course for what was to follow.

Starting was easy. I had no fear of change because I had equipped myself with a powerful force, a foundation of strength, which could not be denied. I discovered a simple secret of life that worked for me. Its meaning was not hidden in metaphors or parables. The truth was contained in a three-word message given to me by my friend, Father John Smyth. The foundation of faith, family and friends gave me a rock upon which to mount my comeback. I was confident that the three Fs, when applied and integrated into my daily existence would literally change my entire life. As it turned out, they did more than change my life… they saved it.

My prayers were focused on asking for the strength to guide me through my present challenge. I believed in my family, who stood beside me throughout the ordeal. I said prayers of thanks for my wife, whose personal faith and inner strength were there to hold everyone else together.

I was also energized by the thousands of cards and letters and the countless messages that were arriving each day from friends and fans who were also praying and pulling for me. It was a flattering and very humbling experience to virtually witness my own memorial service in the media. Months later, I would watch the video accounts of the newscasters and read the seemingly endless inches of copy describing the events. They were filled with varying theories of what actually happened as well as speculations of my future. I thought them to be interesting to watch, knowing that at the time of the incident, nobody could have known how it would all end up. Not even me.

In arming myself for the long battle back, I adopted a motto that said, "Anything worth believing in is worth fighting for." I knew very well that the fight had just begun. While there were lessons being learned with each new day, I laughed as I thought about the most practical lesson of all, told to me in a personal note from a friend, former Chicago hockey writer who wrote... "Always take the valet parking." I appreciated his humor. It gave me a laugh when I needed one.

I recognized that I was truly blessed to have been prepared to meet this incredible challenge and I had been blessed, too, in having the vision to recognize that I needed to take charge of my own life rather than simply allowing myself to be a passive observer in this bizarre drama.

I'm often asked these days whether I consider myself to be blessed or lucky. My answer? Both. I feel greatly blessed and incredibly lucky.

My personal messages continue to grow in strength with every new day of my life. I am consistently challenging myself to make a connection with people who listen to me speak or read my accounts of this and other stories of triumph over adversity. I called upon them to take inventory of their own lives, as I had done. It is often a surprise when people take their first important look in the mirror with complete honesty, only to realize that the image reflecting back at them is truly remarkable.

Understanding the gifts each of us has been given will make us stronger, no matter the magnitude of the challenges that we may be facing. It is our own small treasures that count. Having a clearer image of my own mortality inspired me to never put off the celebration until tomorrow. I've come to realize and accept the fact that the celebration may never come. Of all the implied warranties and guarantees that we think we have in life, tomorrow is not one of them. By appreciating our God-given gifts, we can discover a richer and more fulfilling existence, but we should never take them for granted.

Our daily challenge is to be aware of the fact that these gifts can be taken away as easily as they were given to us. We must frequently remind ourselves that they are fragile, temporary and on loan.

I challenge everyone before whom I speak to take the time to identify the precious gifts in their life. Once discovered, these gifts need to be used, respected and shared with others. If you choose to do this, I honestly believe that each of our lives will be enriched to the point where it will have a more significant meaning for ourselves and for others.

Messmer's Condition Raises Hope

--The Daily Herald

"The future belongs to those who believe in the future of their dreams."
--Eleanor Roosevelt

What So Proudly He Hailed Shooting Victim Able To Sing Again

-- The New York Daily News

"I will sing now… because I can!"
--Wayne Messmer

The Voice of Victory

"O say, you can see, Messmer's on his way back."

The last pitch on this shiny Memorial Day afternoon at Wrigley Field was significant too. Randy Meyers saved a victory by Willy Banks over the Philadelphia Phillies, produced on a ground single. But the Cubs have been alive and well for a couple of weeks, which is why Monday's first pitch soared beyond the scores and highlights as Wayne Messmer went to the mound with a smile on his face and a song in his heart and everyone stood. They always do when this man clears that golden throat to perform The Star Spangled Banner as only he can.

Messmer has lifted more Chicago sports fans out of their seats than any athlete then or now. It will be a while longer until we hear from him. That day shall come, though. He always knew it would.

"Dying was never an option," Messmer said. "Maybe it was my strong faith, my will or maybe it was just plain stupidity. But no, dying was never an option."

Only hours after belting out the National Anthem before a Blackhawks game at The Stadium, Messmer was shot early on Saturday morning, April 9. The bullet entered the left side of his neck; a half inch either way and Messmer would have bled to death or been paralyzed. Even as he drove a couple of blocks to Hawkeye's, the West Side establishment he'd just left, Messmer wondered whether the help he sought could rescue the career he'd built.

"My voice," Messmer said, "That's me. Maybe that's why people have been so kind. If I got shot in the leg, well, I got shot in the leg. But not until the Tuesday after they tell me I was on the operating table for 10 hours did I realize how wonderful these people were. I thought it would be a small news item. I'm a guy who sings the Anthem at hockey games, sings the Anthem and reads the lineups here at Wrigley Field. What followed was unbelievable."

Messmer received boxes of mail, get well wishes from every state in the union, Europe too. He vaguely recalled the saga of Harry Caray the Cubs' Hall of Famer, who suffered a stroke years ago. Caray had propped up many an audience with his genius. When Harry went down, it was time for absolute strangers to return the favor. Caray credits them with his miracle.

Messmer, his pipes still gaining strength beneath that scar, understands now. "They enabled me to keep my spirit and my sense of humor," Messmer said. "When I switched hospitals so I could get my rest, I changed my name to Ralph Kramden. It also proved to my wife, Kathleen, that yeah, I was popular. But, seriously, I believe everything happens for a reason. I feel like I lived through my own funeral and I don't wish that on anyone. Yet, it did show what faith can mean, and I don't mean just mine. I mean the faith of my greatest supporter, my best friend Kathleen. My not singing again was never an option for her. And I will later this summer."

For The Stadium's last regular season Hawks' game ever, Kathleen took Wayne's usual spot in the organ loft. His message to fans was read by broadcaster Pat Foley, also a voice that has warmed many cold winter nights. Then they played The Star Spangled Banner tape and there wasn't a dry eye in the house.

"I was listening in my hospital bed, waiting to go down for a particularly nasty test," Wayne said. "Pat was terrific. The noise was amazing. I haven't yet seen it. Too emotional. Kathleen will get a couple of boxes of Kleenex one night and watch. People associate me with the Anthem and what it represents, and for that, I am honored."

Wayne Messmer thought it would be a nice fit, sneaking into Wrigley Field on Memorial Day, the time to celebrate the fresh air of freedom. "Then all these people came up to see me and hug me," he said. "I figured I'd thank them for all the love. I'm so lucky." Wayne Messmer was back home again at the ballpark, where they were playing his song.

Chapter 14
I'll Take You Home Again Kathleen

No man is capable of climbing a mountain alone. The challenges of our lives come in the daily hurdles we are forced to try to jump over. Sometimes they are higher than our limitations allow us to clear. But with a soulmate, a running partner beside us, it is truly phenomenal to see what we can achieve.

When I truly needed support, I was blessed to have a woman of enormous courage and strength, who looked me squarely in the eye, held my hand and said, "We shouldn't be willing to accept anything less than complete recovery." I could only silently respond with, "Yes, dear." Her confidence and faith were truly inspiring. Even though I had some difficulty trying to convince myself that I could get through the ordeal in one piece, one thing was certain... I could not have done it alone.

Having such a positive partner helped me to fight off the feeling of helplessness almost immediately. It was enormously comforting. We were facing a journey that fell squarely in the "or worse" portion of the wedding vows we had taken years earlier. Less than three months before the incident, we had stood in front of family and friends and reenacted our wedding ceremony and restated our vows – exactly 10 years to the minute from the original ceremony. It was on the precise spot, when the frozen world was shivering on the night of January 14,1994 where time stood still for a moment of togetherness. The future looked so incredibly bright that evening, as if nothing could ever interrupt our celebration. That was then.

Now we're looking at an uphill battle that presented an enormous challenge to the very thing that had brought us together – our music and the ability to sing.

I had walked into a callback audition for a musical production on March 25, 1981 at a rehearsal hall at Sheil Park on Chicago's North Side. The play was Kiss Me Kate, and the lead roles were to be cast. As a baritone who had previously worked for the director, the male lead was something I had already been promised. The female lead, however, was yet to be cast and there were a half-dozen sopranos who were hopeful to get a chance to take part in the production that would be presented at Theatre on the Lake, a Chicago Park District facility situated on a plot of land between Lake Shore Drive and Lake Michigan.

Kathleen would be the actress cast in the part. Almost immediately she won my admiration and respect as a performer and a musician, bringing with her a wealth of stage experience to the role and an aura of professionalism. I immediately discovered that working with her was inspiring.

The show featured the blending of our voices to The Taming Of the Shrew. As we sang the lyrics of the song So in Love in the show, it became obvious that it was describing us. The director had done such a perfect job of casting the two of us as the lead characters of Kate and Petruchio that it extended to our offstage lives as well.

When the production opened in mid-June, it was a sellout for the two-week run of the show. Even after the final chorus had been sung, the casting would stick. No question about it. We were a pair that was meant to be together.

The word was soon out that we were the couple whom our friends would say were "joined at the hip." We laughed about it and it felt as though a new life was emerging from our relationship. The great joy of our lives was sharing the gift of our voices together. We sang with orchestras, in front of choruses, on stage and in concert. The indescribable feeling that we had experienced in performing together was capped off with a duet arrangement of the National Anthem that had gained considerable attention and notoriety for its musical appeal and the unmistakable natural blend of our two voices together.

Other shows were to follow. The Fantasticks, South Pacific, The Music Man, Showboat, A Little Night Music and many other musical reviews. Our voices had become blended in time and had taken on a rich and beautiful musical life, which we truly appreciated and enjoyed sharing. The times we had spent singing together ranked among the most passionate moments of my life. Creating beauty through music with the person you love had emerged as a driving force in both of our lives. Being able to share the gift of our voices with other people made us very aware of the tremendous blessings with which we had been provided. Never a day passed when we failed to recognize the fragile and delicate nature of these precious gifts.

Time and again, the more often we could find the opportunity to sing together, the more often we would do it. It was a feeling of exhilaration to lift our voices in song. The more we sang together, the more in love we seemed to be. "How could this, above all, be taken away from me?" I asked. "How could the most revered of my gifts be stolen?" I didn't care as much that the days of the National Anthem may have ended. I felt that I would have left a good legacy at having done my best for years. But the fear that I may never again have a chance to stand alongside this life partner of mine and make music together was almost too much to bear.

The pain of this thought far suppressed any physical pain I was suffering from the gunshot or the surgery. I knew then, as I know now, that my comeback was singularly fueled by my desire to sing once again with my wife. I would not allow that not to happen.

These dreams and fears were waiting for me each morning as I awoke. Fighting my anxiousness, I had to take things in the order that they came.

First, I had to simply focus my attention on getting well before worrying about carrying a tune. As the hours turned to days and the days into months, our partnership grew stronger by this single focus. It was my job to get well. Kathleen was there every step of the way to cheer me on, to hold my hand when I woke up in the middle of the night with a nightmarish flashback of the split second of terror that had robbed the innocence from the city we so dearly loved.

There had been black tie concerts with symphony orchestras, performances in the rain with the community concert band and all points in between. Whatever the event, if we could sing together, nothing else seemed to matter. I recall the pain in my chest and the tugging at my emotions as I feared that the most important thing in my life was now gone. I knew and could accept that even the applause from the public speaking and concert work might likely have ended with the gunshot. But I was charged by one important desire that no medical exam could determine.

Only someone who has experienced the magnificence of doing what you love and loving what you do could understand and appreciate my motivation. This was much more than my passion. It was a mission, a challenge within me of enormous proportions. I had no assurance that I

164

would be able to speak well enough to resume even a fraction of my career, which had been abruptly put on hold. Yet I looked beyond that hurdle to grab the golden ring.

In my vision, I saw Kathleen standing beside me as I reached deep down inside for the strength to produce the sound that has always been so available to me... to us, before this devastating injury. Never was there a question of if I would blend my voice again with my wife's. The only question was, when?

Individuals who have suffered a major setback in their life can point to a specific driving force that served as their motivation in their return to wholeness. Mine was easily identifiable. It was more specific than just being able to sing again. I was energized by the unquenchable need to sing once again with my beloved Kathleen.

As I sat alone, reflecting the months after the shooting, tranquility took over where the fear subsided. The acceptance of my vision brought on peacefulness unlike anything I had ever experienced. As my life partner, Kathleen, had encouraged and supported, counseled and participated in every aspect of my career, she stood quietly in the shadows as I was illuminated in the spotlight. She did so with the confidence of a person with great inner strength and personal conviction. Her unselfishness had never gone unnoticed. She seemed to always be shining through with tremendous brilliance when it came to the day-to-day task of trying to get over one hurdle at a time. When my patience was failing, which happened with regularity, I would turn to her and draw strength from the fact that her purpose in life seemed to allow her the gift of being able to visualize beyond the pain, to look ahead at what will be, instead of dwelling on what we had apparently lost.

Her attitude was captured in the lyrics of a pop song that stated, "Nobody's gonna break-a my stride. Nobody's gonna slow me down. O, no... I've got to keep on moving." This became her theme song during the tumultuous days after I was hurt and during the critical first days when the question of what would become of her husband was still yet to be answered. There had been no better example of her resolve than the night of April 14, 1994.

The night of the Chicago Stadium farewell. It was on that night when she stood up and was recognized as a person of unconquerable spirit as she was proudly poised and sang through her tears, singing proudly as I lay in the hospital, just days after the shooting. Kathleen had agreed to go to the Stadium that night for one reason: to bring back the feelings of the evening, to recall them to me later. Her presence was magical, even legendary. She displayed to the rest of the world what I already knew. We've got to keep on moving! She left an unforgettable image in the minds and hearts of thousands of people who saw her standing in the organ loft on the very spot where I had stood for 13 glorious seasons.

Her voice rang out with the beauty of an angel as this devoted and loving wife sang along with the recorded voice of her injured husband. She sang triumphantly with tears of courage streaming down her cheeks. Despite the fact that she held no microphone, it seemed as though everyone in the building and everyone listening on the broadcast could sense and hear her angelic voice as well as her pain and anguish, simply through her presence. They also felt her love and were inspired by it.

She was a living example of how to face adversity by standing up strong with courage and dignity. The overflow crowd swelled up with emotion as the drama unfolded before them. No one who was there or who saw the video account of the event will ever forget the sight of the courageous wife who refused to give up, despite the odds.

As I lay still in the hospital that night, I realized that I could not have been prouder of my wife at any moment that I have ever known her, as I was right then.

We were still six months away from what would become the night when The Voice of Victory would be heard once again. Neither of us had any way of knowing what the future held in store. We only knew that we were going to continue to try. Whatever doubts were lingering in my mind were lessened just knowing that I had the support and love of this wonderful friend in my life. The feeling of peace was getting closer as we worked our way through this nightmare. The comfort came in knowing that whatever the end result would be, we would come through it together.

It would be almost a year after the event before the two of us were able to sit down together and watch a video of that evening. When we did, nestled close to each other in a remote log cabin in Door County, WI, the feelings came back just as intensely as they had been on that memorable night. As we held on to each other, the gratitude heavily outweighed the sadness. We had conquered the fears and had emerged with the knowledge of intense appreciation for each other. Our partnership had been tested, as had our resilience, and we stood up to it.

As a result of our prayers and support, we had seen each other emerge from the darkness into a brilliant future together. We were grateful for, yet humbled by, the mercy and grace of which we had been showered. We had always been accused of being overly romantic, which was fine with us. Perhaps an indication of just how sentimental we are came when we took my wedding ring back to the jeweler for repairs after it had been cut off in the emergency room to accommodate the swelling in my finger. My ring needed to be melted down and reshaped.

Kathleen's was slightly too large, so we decided to have the jeweler take some gold out from her ring and use it to repair mine. The recrafted wedding rings we now wore carried with them an even richer sense of sentiment and emotion. As we held hands to watch the special moment from Chicago Stadium, we couldn't help but recognize the intensity with which our lives had been interwoven.

Not a single day goes by without me thanking God for placing this amazing person beside me in my life. Her talents as an actress and musician are rivaled only by her gift of working with children. All of her collective talents are overshadowed by her sense of compassion and warmth.

As the Pride of the Yankees, Lou Gehrig, said so eloquently in his farewell address to the nation on July 4, 1939 before an adoring crowd at Yankee Stadium and for the millions of fans who listened on radio, "I consider myself the luckiest man on the face of the Earth. And, I may have been given a bad break, but I've got an awful lot to live for." I enthusiastically agree. Although I consider myself to be blessed as well as lucky.

I know without question that I, too, have an awful lot to live for. I've been given the gift of an angel named Kathleen.

Wolves Are Set To Howl
Messmer, Expected Sellout welcome IHL To Chicago

--The Chicago Sun-Times

"Trust in God. Believe in yourself. Dare to dream."
--Dr. Robert Schuller

Wayne Messmer
Comeback Of The Year

--The Chicago Sun-Times

*"Life loves to be taken by the lapel and told
'I am with you, kid. Let's go' "*
--Dr Maya Angelou

Chapter 15

Let the Howling Begin

October 14, 1994

Of course, I knew the tune. I had sung it so many times before. Yet I had always approached the event with a comfort level and a sense of confidence. This, however, was a very different experience for me. My concern was on several levels as it related to the upcoming minute-and-a -half, now just a few hours away. What if I blow it? What then?

I knew that everyone would be watching and waiting to hear my voice. I entertained the fear that the same fans who had been so warm and supportive throughout the years might change their feelings if they discovered that I just couldn't do it anymore.

Sitting in a nearby hotel suite, I looked out the window to the Rosemont Horizon (Allstate Arena) where the event would soon take place. I was still deciding the critical details that were just ahead of me. The suit I would wear, my time of arrival, the words I would say when asked the question, "How do you feel?" I still didn't know. Maybe it wouldn't feel good. If it sounded horrible, I knew I would feel as thought I'd cheated the thousands of supporters who had rallied around me for this very moment. I was tormenting myself with a series of second-guesses.

The biggest question of all was simply, "Could I sing well enough to pass the test?" I tried vocalizing a few notes earlier in the day only to discover that my throat was tight, and the sensation was anything but natural or comfortable. I was scared, and I was also scarred.

At one point in the afternoon, I drove over to the building and did what needed to be done. A sound check where I would test the level of the microphone and adjust it to my voice. To me, a sound check had always been rather routine. You simply sing a couple notes and give a nod. Occasionally, but rarely, a tweak or two would get the sound just as I liked it.

I knew that no equalizer or audio mixing board could help me as much as I needed to be helped. I wanted the old voice back. For me, it had always been as easy as falling off a log for all those years. I would just take a deep breath, open my mouth and start to sing. It was as simple as that. Not tonight though. I was going to have to work and work hard.

Stepping onto the ice, I clutched the microphone and tried to act very relaxed. "No big deal," I kept telling myself. As the sound technician called to me for a test, "Check one!" I bellowed in my best PA Announcer's voice. I was just stalling. I knew it and so did everyone else in the building.

Finally, the moment had arrived. It was the position I had visualized of being at the end of the high diving board, where I now realized that I had come too far to turn back now. "O, say can you see?" I shouted somewhat on pitch. Not enough to decide the crucial settings and adjustments that needed to be made. However, I was asked to repeat it. "That wasn't too bad," I thought. I hadn't noticed anyone turning and laughing or, worse, standing there with a stunned look on his or her face. I revved up, took a big gasp and let a few more notes fly. "For the land of the free!" I sang, gaining confidence with each new note.

"That will be fine," I said into the microphone, recreating the familiar sound of a voice that had taken me so far in my career. It bore a close resemblance to the same voice that had been stolen from me. It had now been returned once again as a gift.

I thought back to a morning no more than two weeks earlier when I had summoned Kathleen to the piano before she went off to her teaching job. I plunked out a C-sharp and looked at her invitingly and said, "Let's do it." To which she responded with a rather inquisitive look. "I mean, let's try to do the tune," I said.

She knew that I meant the duet arrangement of the National Anthem that we had sung dozens of times before. As we started to sing, the room lit up with hope as it filled with our voices. We concluded with a kiss and then held each other for several minutes. "We're going to do this," I said, exhibiting a new confidence. "I knew it all along," she said to me with a smile that was worthy of the cover of *Life Magazine.* That memory was as intense in my mind as the moment it happened as I tried to gather all the courage I could for the event that was now just a couple of hours away.

I needed to think. I needed to pray. I needed to be alone.

The night was not just about me, by any means. It was the start of a new and exciting professional team for the city. The Chicago Wolves Professional Hockey Team and I were sharing the spotlight that night and I couldn't have picked a more deserving partner.

It was the opening night of a whole new show, a world premiere, featuring a talented supporting cast of some hard working and dedicated front office people, a collection of veterans and some young, hopeful professional hockey players, and tagging along was a bruised Anthem singer on center stage.

My involvement with the Wolves had evolved from a conversation at Chicago Stadium with Grant Mulvey, one-time Chicago Blackhawks star who was rumored to be involved with a startup of a new sports venture. It was the fall of 1993. Even then, I was always on the lookout for new and challenging opportunities. If it sounded interesting, I was willing to take a look at a new project. Well, this one did.

Knowing the Chicago sports market fairly well, I managed to express my interest in being a part of the new team. "I'll call you," Mulvey said, but I figured he probably wouldn't. To my surprise, when the phone rang the next day, the conversation began. Hours of discussions ultimately led to a face-to-face meeting with the ownership group. I remember taking them through the process of trying to convince them that I had the experience and contacts to help guide the group through the process of achieving what they were setting out to do. They had the faith that I was the right guy and hired me to take over the role of Executive Vice President.

It was interesting that the early plans were for a team that was to be considerably different than the production which was to be staged this evening. Initially, the Chicago Wolves were on the drawing board as a professional roller hockey team. A new league had been established – Roller Hockey International, RHI – and Chicago would be the latest expansion team. My job was to assemble a staff whose assignment it would be to market and promote this new team.

Much to the surprise of the newly formed staff, after spending months in preparation for the project, the entire focus was shifted from roller hockey to ice hockey. The team would still be known as the Wolves, but this was to be an entirely different game. The work was about to begin.

From the day I was first introduced to Don Levin until we stood together on a sold out opening night, it was less than a year. We had spent so much time together in the building process, taking it from the ground up, that we had virtually lived nothing but Wolves Hockey for the past year. It was an amazing learning experience.

Don had been enormously supportive during my time of recovery. From the very moment when I was hurt, he was ready to provide anything my family or I might need to get through the tragedy. He had personally sent my sister, Barb, a plane ticket to come to Chicago from her home in Albuquerque to be with me in the hospital. A large part of my motivation for selecting this particular night for my triumphant return on the stage of the Chicago Wolves and not a Cubs or Blackhawks game can be directly attributed to my appreciation and loyalty to him. He was then, and continues today, to be a dear and loyal friend.

True, the Cubs had called off their season with the player strike for the summer of 1994 and the 'Hawks had been shut out by the owner's lockout, which would delay their season opener until January 1995. But it was a simple matter of respect that made me come to understand that I had selected the right stage for this important event in my life.

Perhaps aiding in the choice of the comeback, in contrast, not a single representative or owner from the Blackhawks' organization ever personally contacted me directly, either by phone or message throughout the ordeal.

Don Levin also came to display a genuine concern for the fans from the very beginning. This trait continued to grow over the years from one season to the next. I was then, and am now, genuinely glad that this historic night was taking place with the Chicago Wolves Hockey Team.

Before the Major League players' strike took the game away from the fans that summer, I was able to capture a day to remember in the friendly confines. The day came on May 30, 1994 when, without advance notice or any fanfare, Kathleen and I decided we wanted to be fans and just see a ballgame. I would not be there to sing or announce, but rather to take my first step back into the environment I had called home for so many years.

I called to let a few people know that we would be there. The Cubs marketing department, well known for never letting an opportunity for a celebration or photo opp pass them by, set the table for a homecoming.

Later, the Cubs informed me that they would've continued to pay me for the summer's work had it not been for the player's strike, even though I would have obviously not been able to fulfill my duties. A lovely gesture for which I was appreciative, (although the strike cancelled that offer).

Cubs' management also decided to fly the flag with the initials WM over the press box area, immediately above where I sat for 10 seasons, as a symbol of support for my recovery. Another beautiful getsure.

It was ironic that I happened to return to Wrigley Field on the same day when the photo playing cards displaying my picture were supposed to be passed out to the fans as a promotional item. It was quite a tribute, even though the cards never made it into the hands of the fans.

Upon arrival at the park, I was whisked upstairs and quickly booked as the guest for the on-field lead-off man pre-game TV show. I was also penciled in as the surprise guest to throw out a ceremonial first pitch and also promised to visit the WGN radio booth during the game.

It was a day I would always remember. I was so grateful to be there at all, but still a long way from being back. Although that would not be the day, I knew that the time would eventually come when I could once again proudly take the steps out to my position in front of the Cubs' dugout and honor America with a song that meant so much to me.

I prayed again for the patience to guide me toward the arrival of that day. On that sunny afternoon at Wrigley Field, I was still five months away from the moment when I would take the microphone and sing again. This was a day to relax and enjoy.

Now that moment was here. An hour away until I would sing again. Just as I had not allowed one minute of the experience at the Cubs' game to pass without the highest degree of thanks, I would not let one second of the evening ahead happen without absorbing it all.

I knew that someday soon it would be time to sing a hymn of praise to the great country that we live in and to our merciful Lord who demanded an encore that I would gladly perform.

That was still in the future of the spring and summer months ahead. In the meantime, I had work to do immediately in front of me that night. After adjusting the knot in my tie, I was ready to take the five-minute drive to the place where we could make some history.

Nancy Faust, Chicago's legendary sports organist and long-time musical star of the Chicago White Sox had been hired to play for the Wolves' opening night. It meant that my old friend would accompany me in what I hoped would be the first of many more Anthems. She was there when I entered the building, and so was the press, who were there out in full force.

It seems as though everybody wanted a piece of my story, a quote, a reaction and another recap of what it means to me to be singing again. I still didn't know. I hadn't sung yet.

Cameras were shoved in my face and well-meaning reporters were ready to capture my first words to help them get an indication of how I felt at that very moment. I could only say that, if anything, if felt strange. Oh, sure, I was getting the starting assignment, but I was used to being an all-star. This was very different for me. I felt as if I used to be a right hander and now I was going to be forced to throw as a southpaw. Things were more than just different, they were all-together brand new. It had been anything but easy just preparing myself to get to that point at all. The anxiousness intensified as it got closer to game time.

It was now 6:30 p.m. The teams were ready to take to the ice for their warm-ups and the fans were filling the arena by the hundreds. After what seemed like a lifetime, the moment finally arrived. The lights were dimmed, and the player introductions began. There were laser lights and fireworks. It was a celebration. The roar of the crowd sounded so familiar, so natural. Fans were howling as if it had been rehearsed many times before, yet it was the first ever home game for the brand-new Chicago Wolves.

At 7:37 p.m., Ed Vucinic, the Wolves PA announcer read from the script:

"Six months ago, his voice was silenced. Tonight, he's back."

He paused as the crowd roared its approval. He continued:

"Ladies and gentlemen, please rise as we honor America. Accompanied by Nancy Faust at the organ, please join Wayne Messmer with the singing our National Anthem."

This was the dream. It was exactly what I had visualized hundreds of times from the first moment of consciousness after I realized that I had lived through the shooting and the surgery. It was the magical and miraculous moment for which I had prayed.

The noise level was intense with thunderous applause. I could feel the collective energy of the fans who had wished as hard as they could to make this moment happen. "The Guy Who Sings the Anthem" was about to recapture the magic that had been robbed and had been feared to have been lost forever. Tonight, it was about to be found again. I sensed the intensity and made the Sign of the Cross, saying a short prayer asking for help to get through the song. I also offered a prayer of thanks for allowing me to just make it back to the spotlight, no matter what would happen from this point on.

As the decibel level climbed higher, it was time to take the walk on the red carpet that had been rolled out on the ice for the event. I knew that in many ways I could not take the walk alone. I also knew that the lessons I had learned showed me that I could never imagine walking alone again. I had beaten the odds and I was there to collect my winnings. The song was my payoff for all the hard work we had done. The night was no longer just a faint hope. It was now something we could touch.

I took Kathleen's hand and started the journey as I proudly made my way out to my mark. She looked at me, wondering why I wanted her to be on the ice with me. There was no question that she had been my strength and had never asked for a thing. Tonight, she was going to share the spotlight. It was an honor that she deserved, perhaps much more than myself. I made the promise that she would never again be left in my shadow.

As I took her hand in mine, I didn't realize that I was literally holding on for dear life. Of course, she never complained. Knowing that the time had come, we started out on the 30-foot walk that seemed like a half mile. I could only imagine how hard I was squeezing her hand. It was probably numb by the time we hit the end of the carpet. I often tease her to this day, asking if she has finally regained full feeling in her hand.

The familiar eight-bar introduction began on the organ, as I took a deep breath, hoped for the best and began to sing. The words were familiar, and the intense emotion was nearly overwhelming. This was a singular instant in my life where I felt the brilliance of the spotlight needed to be savored and enjoyed. I've since mentioned to people that if they ever wondered what the voice of the Holy Spirit sounds like, they need not look any further than my performance on that evening. October 14, 1994. "He's a baritone," I tell them with no uncertainty.

As my mouth opened, the sound triumphantly emerged, I knew it was different, yet it sounded enough like the old Wayne for everyone in the building – as well as those that were watching on TV and listening on the radio – to comment that, "Wayne was back." The song reached its crescendo and the words "Land of the free and home of the brave," finished with a collective explosion of cheers and tears among the 17,000 fans who had done their part and helped make this night unforgettable.

Kathleen shouted with joy as I completed this historic performance. Her screams of delight were echoed by my family who was assembled in the stands and by the thousands of fans who, for that one amazing moment in time, all bonded to make a statement that we had beaten the odds together. The prayers had indeed been answered.

The voice would progressively get better in time, but for now it served its purpose well. I was on top of the world. I had survived, had come back to sing again and had lived to talk about my experience. I sang that night for the other people who had been shot in Chicago the same weekend as I had. I sang cast in the role of a victor not a victim. I had fought so terribly hard to be ready when the opportunity arose so that I would be able to shout, "We can't let the bad guys win!"

As we walked off the red carpet, a group of reporters was there to capture our immediate reaction. I joked later that when asked, "What are you going to do now?" I should have answered, "I'm going to Disneyworld!" I could have probably gotten a commercial out of the deal, but that was okay. What I did get from that night was priceless. I got my life back.

One comment drew attention to the foundation of my faith that had carried me back to the moment. I said that I felt that if the ice had melted, I would have been able to walk on water. The words signified that the Lord had given me this magnificent gift and had taken it back. But now, I've publicly acknowledged that it was only with His blessing that the gift had been restored.

The entire evening was truly overwhelming. It was the most humbling moment of my life. A moment and a feeling I will never allow myself to forget. All the tears, the doubts, the talks to myself in the months after the shooting where I was absolutely convinced that I would never see this night were all washed away in a whirlwind of joy.

The rest of the evening was pure celebration. I recall in particular the excitement of my younger sister, Tina who, as a singer herself, could truly understand the importance of music in my life. She celebrated abundantly with me, as did the rest of my family and friends who had chosen to share in this triumphant moment.

The Wolves skated their way to a victory that night – a 4-2 win over the Detroit Vipers. It was a night of hockey where the excitement was rivaled just four years later in the same building when the same two teams squared off in the seventh and deciding game of the Turner Cup Championship Series, also won by the Wolves. This time by a 3-0 score. The emotions were intense from start to finish. I signed autographs by the hundreds. It was a night that I described as an Elvis experience, being shadowed all evening by three bodyguards.

The party after the game was back at the same hotel suite where I had managed to direct the butterflies in my stomach to fly in formation. Again, it was Kathleen who captured the moment with a gift that has provided joy and inspiration to me every day since. She handed me a picture of the great Lou Gehrig, standing at home plate at Yankee Stadium on July 4, 1939 as he bid farewell to his beloved fans. The picture's unique feature was that it talked. When you pressed a button that was built into the frame, the unmistakable voice of "The Iron Horse," "The Pride of the Yankees" was heard with all his spirit coming through each spoken word. I welcomed the encore of his inspirational message, bellowing more loudly than I had ever heard them before:

"...I consider myself the luckiest man on the face of the earth. And I may have been given a bad break, but I've got an awful lot to live for."

~ Lou Gehrig

Once again, I found it rather natural to relate to his message. It instantly became my personal message as well. I knew without any doubt that I too had an awful lot to live for. I'd always considered myself a lucky man, but now I was also aware of just how blessed I was.

Despite the return to singing, my work was far from done. In fact, in many ways it had just begun. *The Voice of Victory* had answered a date with destiny.

I reached out once again and took Kathleen's hand after everyone had gone home. Whereupon both of us sighed a breath of relief, knowing that we had taken these enormous steps together. We had taken the journey one step, one day at a time. I said a solemn prayer of thanks. We slept well that night with peaceful dreams.

Our dreams were not of what had been, but of what was yet to come. Somehow, I just knew it would be great.

Messmer, Wolves 'Hits'

--*The Chicago Tribune*

"Opportunity often comes in the form of misfortune, or temporary defeat."
--Napoleon Hill

Messmer Upstages
Wolves In Opener

--The Chicago Sun-Times

"Many people will tell you why something cannot be done, you only require one reason - your own - to succeed."
--Wayne Messmer

Chapter 16
After The Ball Is Over

I looked at Kathleen the day after the inaugural Chicago Wolves hockey game and said, "Now what?" It was a question that needed to be asked. There would be assumptions and expectations, many of which may or may not be true or accurate. Was everything as good as new? Did all the king's horses and all the king's men put Humpty Dumpty back together again?

I knew the answer was no. Things were different. There was still a lot of healing to do physically and mentally. I also recognized a sense of an emotional letdown in almost a melancholy way. Throughout all the trying months that had passed since the moment when I sat on the examining table at the hospital with needles sticking out of my throat, there had been flashes of joy and disappointment. There had also been moments of terror and depression, coupled with the oppressive feeling of loss. How could I step forward and tell the same people who had cheered me on that I had changed, as had my priorities in life?

Some of these changes would be made much easier by the actions and reactions of those very people with whom I had been associated. I couldn't help but equate my situation with that of the Marathon runner who trains so passionately for the grueling 26-mile event. He works every day in his disciplined manner to bring himself to the point of being ready to be in the moment of the competition, of the performance. In many ways, I had done that as well. My countless hours of self-administered physical therapy and musical reeducation of the muscles in my throat were similar to the training of the marathoner. But now I had finished the race and I was not sure that I wanted to run it again.

I had been so singularly focused on coming back, just once, that the thought of resuming the maddening schedule and the hectic pace I had been on prior to my injury posed a less than attractive picture to me. In my work as a professional speaker in the corporate and association world, I often tell the wonderful story of the athlete who inspired many people in the 1968 Mexico City Olympic Games.

Here was a marathon runner from Tanzania, there with a purpose, that he made very clear to anyone who would listen and understand. He got his chance to tell his story to the great interviewer Bud Greenspan, who conducted the up-close-and-personal profile of a man who spoke from his heart.

The athlete continued to run the race long after the rest of the field had completed the journey. In fact, he was the last athlete to finish the marathon. He pushed on even though it had been well over an hour since the first runners had entered the stadium and took their final lap on the track before crossing the finish line. The runner had fallen and had injured himself in a collision with another athlete. Out of the darkness came this man of determination, of impressive courage and will. His appearance caught the attention of the small crowd who was still remaining, but they watched him struggle through each step, in a painful, yet purposeful manner. Inching closer and closer to his goal. Soon, the crowd began to sense the passion of this man. They could recognize that if all else had collapsed around him, he would still continue to run toward the finish line.

Gradually, the cheering began to swell until all of those were present stood up in support to holler their encouragement. The doubts had evolved into applause and the comedy had transformed into drama. As he crossed the finish line, the crowd erupted in delight that they had been privileged enough to witness a dream, not merely an athletic event.

The question begged to be asked, "Why did you continue when you knew there was no chance of winning, no chance of finishing anywhere near the top of the field?" Greenspan probed and the answer he received has always stuck in my mind. As the words of a man with integrity as well as with courage, he told how he had come from a poor, small village where many people had sacrificed many things so that he could be there.

He went on to describe his country of Tanzania as an impoverished nation of limited means. But he spoke with passion as he said a rather amazing statement of purpose, telling everyone who would listen exactly why he had never stopped running.

His words cut to the truth when he said that all of the sacrifices made by those good people who sent him 5,000 miles, to finish the race, not just to start it.

Those words made me wonder. Had I finished my race? Or had I just started it? The playing conditions had been changed. The ease with which I had been able to cross the finish line so many times in the past was now much more difficult. My fears, to some extent, had been realized. Yes, my voice sounded virtually the same as it had been before the injury. But the truth was, it had become considerably more physically demanding to produce the same quality of sound. Only I knew that secret.

The NHL owners' lockout had canceled the start of the Blackhawks season, which, by the way, was to have begun 12 days prior to the spectacular night of the Wolves' premiere showing. They were to eventually settle the labor dispute in

188

time to schedule their home opening night for January 25, 1995.

This would be the first ever regular season game in the sparkling new United Center. Its location was immediately across the street from the venerable old Chicago Stadium, which had been ceremoniously laid to rest and had felt the blows of the wrecking ball. The remnants of the Stadium were still visible as the demolition of this once proud structure took place in the shadows of the much larger state-of-the-art venue.

I was anxiously excited to have the opportunity to return into the presence of the 'Hawks fans, with whom I had shared some of my most thrilling sports and musical memories that filled my crowded scrapbook. Before I would have that chance, the Chicago Bulls invited Kathleen and I to perform the National Anthem at their inaugural regular season NBA game at the new arena.

On November 4, 1994 we stepped to center court and sang the very song that we had cried over less than six weeks earlier when we had discovered in a most private moment in our home that we could indeed sing again. It was another entry into a series of electric moments as the crowd responded with the same level of appreciation that was shown to the marathon runner, John Stephen Akhwari of Tanzania in Mexico City. They also knew I had come to finish the song, not just start it.

One week prior to the Hawks' opening night in late January 1995, I was summoned to the team's office where I was called to a meeting with the General Manager. I knew something was going on, since in the 13 full seasons I had been the National Anthem soloist, I had never before been summoned to the front office.

I was informed in a brief and rather casual meeting that the established Blackhawks organization viewed the upstart Chicago Wolves – which by this time had played 21 of their scheduled 41 home games – as competition, and I was told that they considered my involvement with the Wolves to be, "A conflict of interest." And the statement concluded with, "So, we're going to have to let you go."

"Just like that?" I thought. After 13 seasons of setting the table for all of those battles, I was being dismissed without an opportunity to present my own defense? Actually, I found the statement to be a compliment since the Wolves had only been in business for four months at that point. I also had to admit that I was taken aback by the logic of their decision regarding the claim of "conflict of interest." I was the singer of the National Anthem, which had no proprietary ownership by any sports team.

It was also my theory, which has since proven to be true, that the Wolves of the then International Hockey League and eventually the American Hockey League, would help to introduce a new market of fans to professional hockey by providing an affordable opportunity for families. These fans, in turn, would eventually come to support the Blackhawks of the National Hockey League as well. From my perspective, the Wolves had taken a giant step forward to promote the sport of hockey in Chicago and have continued to do so ever since. Obviously, we did not mutually agree on that perspective.

Our conversation concluded abruptly once the message was delivered. I said right then that I was still interested in continuing the relationship and was prepared to do so, should they change their minds. I agreed to not comment about the fact that I had been dismissed until after I sang for what would be the final time for the Hawks at their opening night game, now less than a week away.

The organization prepared a statement and informed the media that we had come to terms with the separation by "mutual agreement," effective on opening night. It was more of what I would call a "mutual understanding." They understood that I would no longer be allowed to continue singing there and I understood that I had been fired.

I never did sign off on the prepared press release. Since I wanted to continue in my role, but I also did not want to be anywhere that I was no longer welcomed.

Opening night at the United Center January 25, 1995

It should have been a banner night. It was, instead, an evening filled with mixed emotions. The best part of the event was that the most important people were there: the fans. They responded as they always had in the past, screaming their lungs out and clapping throughout the singing of O, Canada and the Star Spangled Banner. They momentarily brought the magic from the revered Chicago Stadium to life in "The New Place" as many people were already calling it.

Upon arrival at the arena, I picked up my two tickets for the night at the front desk, at which point I probably should have recognized the indication that the organization was just going through the motions, allowing me to sing one last time. I looked at the tickets in near disbelief. Kathleen and I were exiled into the distant heights of one of the farthest sections possible. I didn't know whether to laugh or to cry.

It was tragically comic. We never did go to those seats. Instead, we were invited to watch the game from the vantage point of the suite owned by Don Levin, the owner of the

Chicago Wolves hockey team. I couldn't help but notice the statements that were being made by the set of circumstances which occurred throughout the course of the evening and the night had just begun.

Another genuine disappointment also came on the ice after I had finished singing that night. The opponent was the Edmonton Oilers, a team with which the 'Hawks had played some very physical games over the years. After I was through with the emotionally draining performance of the Anthems, a number of visiting players banged their sticks on the ice, showing their approval. We made eye contact and nodded their heads before the opening face off as a final salute to someone they had known for 13 years. To my disappointment, not a single member of my home team made the slightest effort whatsoever. The joy of the moment was dampened with sadness. Considering the situation, I could never understand that coldness. After singing, I stepped onto the concourse of the new facility and spoke to the press. I restated that I was interested in continuing to sing for the organization and I would eagerly accept their invitation, should it come. It never did.

Despite the unfortunate circumstances of that one evening, I remained eternally grateful to have been able to sing in that situation for 13 seasons. It was something that I knew most people would love to have done just once in their life. Still I couldn't seem to be able to completely erase the fact that I was saddened that the tradition had come to an end without the courtesy of a farewell handshake.

My comments that night were truthful and sincere. I said that I had 13 years of absolute magic there. I was a second balcony guy who was given a talent to sing the Anthem for the country I love, in the city in which I was born, for a team I had followed since I was a kid. Am I angry? No. Am I bitter? No. What I am is sad and disappointed.

We parted friends and we continue as such. We've known each other too long to end that friendship, I said. But I couldn't shake the feeling that my friend had really let me down.

I came to realize that things change, sometimes unexpectedly and in ways that we cannot possibly anticipate. I continue to this day to cherish the long relationship I had with the organization and I felt especially privileged to have had such a wonderful relationship with the fans, a relationship that has transcended beyond hockey games and those unforgettable moments at Chicago Stadium into all other areas of my life.

A rather interesting thing developed a few weeks later when I was invited to come to St. Louis to sing for the opening of the newly renovated Kiel Center on February 9, 1995. It was to be a ceremonious event. The game featured a familiar opponent, which was none other than the Chicago Blackhawks. I viewed the occasion as a tremendous compliment; to be invited to sing in the arena of an opponent who, for years, had been intimidated in Chicago Stadium by the intensity of the crowd's response during the National Anthem prior to games there.

It was exactly 10 months to the day since I had been shot. To me, it was a significant opportunity to do what I love to do. I was flattered to have been asked and I graciously accepted the invitation. I made it clear to the Blues' organization that I was not there on this one time only appearance to attempt to humiliate or embarrass the Blackhawks. My motivation for standing there on the ice to sing was purely personal.

I was not so naïve to not recognize the fact that the invitation for me to be there had personally come from Mike Keenan, then the coach of the St. Louis team and the former General Manager/Head Coach of the Hawks. Keenan, like myself, had also been dismissed in Chicago and was a man who may have had a statement to make. I didn't question anyone else's agenda. That was their business.

I had always been a 'Hawks fan and always would be. Despite the possible motivations for the St. Louis organization inviting me, my reason to be there was much simpler. I didn't feel the slightest need to have to explain my presence. I wanted to sing... because I could.

I was treated royally and made to feel at home. The St. Louis hockey crowd, while very excitable, had never developed the level of intensity and boisterousness outbursts of emotion for the Nation Anthem as had the 'Hawks fans in their unique fashion. That night would be different. They imitated their Chicago counterparts by hollering, shouting and clapping from start to finish. From the second I was introduced until the final strains of the song, it was fun. It seemed natural. It fit like a well-worn sneaker. I was performing at the big-league level, being recognized for my ability to sing... a craft that I had worked so very hard to recapture – and the crowd responded.

While still on the ice after the music had ended, and even before the cheering had subsided, I was surprised to hear the comments made to me by a couple of players wearing the visiting red sweater. As I was still enjoying the moment, the two biggest names of the Chicago team, assuming a stance they probably perceived as loyalty to the organization, skated passed me just close enough to shout obscenities. Had it not been so childish and rather pathetic, I might have been upset by it. To me, it was a perfect example of what happens when comments are made without first making any effort to understand the truth.

I found it interesting that within a matter of a couple years, both of these individuals, who had portrayed themselves as "company men," were wearing the colors of different teams. They, too, it seemed had responded to the opportunity to exhibit their professional skills elsewhere when their services were no longer wanted, precisely as I had done that very night in St. Louis. Their unfortunate comments made me feel more embarrassed for them than anything else.

Life after the one-night stand in St. Louis continued to unveil opportunities in and outside of sports. I had revisited the period of my life from where I first began as a singer and announcer, trying to determine the course of where I would be called. The Cubs had been understanding enough to allow our relationship to take on a new role – that of National Anthem soloist only. After some soul-searching analysis, I decided that the rigors of the everyday demands on my voice would simply had been too much.

I returned to sing again at Wrigley Field on opening day 1995, experiencing a moment that had served as an inspirational goal during my entire period of injury and recovery. I've since maintained a schedule of Anthem appearances with the Cubs each year since then, including opening day and a good number of other selected home games throughout the summer. This ongoing relationship has afforded me the chance to continue to sing before the incredibly loyal fans in the most beautiful ballpark in baseball. A few years later, I would return for another run of several seasons in the PA Announcer's role.

Each time I'm introduced to speak as well as sing, whether it is in front of 40,000 people, a national convention or a small gathering at a business meeting, I still recognize how tremendously blessed I am being able to continue with my life through the use of my voice. There have been repeated times when I've opened my mouth to absolute amazement that I am able to even speak. The miracle of having my singing voice restored still makes me eternally grateful.

I can recall on numerous occasions when, in the midst of singing on a particularly beautiful day at the ballpark, I sense an almost out of body experience as I hear a voice emerging from me that, in so many ways, has no business being there – except to say that I still have it so that it can be utilized for a lot of work that is yet to be done with it.

The, "Why did I get better?" question becomes more obvious to me with each opportunity to speak or sing. I feel compelled to tell the story of my recovery. As a Certified Professional Speaker (CSP) as designated by the National Speakers Association, I have the occasion to stand before thousands of people each year. I continue to tell this and other stories, recognizing that these words can and do touch the lives of other people who have had similar setbacks in their lives. Having been affected by injury, serious illness, accidents, untruths or unkind words being said to or about them.

Despite the adversity, the only way out is through forgiveness. I carry no anger, no bitterness and no sense of revenge or regret in my personal or professional life. My mission has become very clear. I continue to work toward the goal of connecting with as many individuals as I possibly can through the message of my words and through my music. An underlying statement in my signature story is that we can never allow the bad guys to win. Whatever the cost, we must continue to set the course to see that good will triumph over evil.

Why did I get better? I no longer have to ask that question. I now know the answer. I got better to be able to tell this story.

Wayne Messmer

On January 25, 1995
Steve Rosenbloom wrote in The Chicago Sun-Times

Messmer's Final Notes a Star-Spangled Shame

O, say can you see? No, frankly, I can't. I can't see the point. I can't understand the reason. I can't imagine a Blackhawks game without Wayne Messmer doing the Anthem. All I can see is that the atmosphere of hockey night in Chicago just turned as painful as the Hawks' special teams. But apparently, that's the deal.

There will be a hockey game in the United Center tonight and Messmer will be there, singing the way he used to before he took a bullet to the throat in the horrible incident last April that didn't just threaten his career, but his life.

Then, that's it. A twilight's last gleaming. A local institution is done. A civic treasure ripped from us. Make that another civic treasure. First Ditka, then Jordan, then any thought of another Bulls championship. Just spray paint the Art Institute lions and finish the job, why don't you? Doesn't anybody understand? Messmer was a major reason to attend a Hawks game. Sometimes the only reason since he first brought the golden pipes to the game in 1981. Everyone in the city knows it. Everyone in hockey knows it. Heck, most of North America knows it after his heart-tugging rendition at the 1991 All-Star Game just days after the Gulf War broke out. You could have cried then, you want to now.

Ever since that memorable playoff game in 1985 against Edmonton – ironically tonight's opponent – fans would stand and clap even before the organ plinked out a couple of notes. Then they would cheer, louder than most buildings just to start with. By the time we go around to, "O'er the land of the free," forget it. The place was nutso, and we had to take his word that he was still actually singing at the end.

Now he won't be. "Gave proof through the night that our flag was still there." How did this happen? Well, we still don't know for sure. The Hawks' press release simply said that Messmer will no longer

198

continue his duties as soloist, but he agreed to come back and sing at the opening night. No, sorry. That doesn't explain why the baritone of the Blue Line has been iced.

"The release was a release we mutually agreed upon," Hawks spokesman said. "Wayne knows our feelings towards him and we know Wayne's feelings toward us. We have a friendship that will continue."

Look, if it was mutual, why wouldn't Messmer talk about it Tuesday instead of waiting until after he sings tonight. Boy, this looks fishy. Not to mention petty. So, the temptation is to blame someone here. Like the Hawks. Isn't just like them? An outfit that fired Coach Billy Reay by shoving his pink slip under the door on Christmas Eve and fired Mike Keenan as General Manager because he had the gall to act like a General Manager. We could speculate to that point, especially with Messmer being a high muckamuck with the minor league Wolves. Hey, they're encroaching on the disposable hockey income that the Hawks used to monopolize. You know how Bill Wirtz feels about cash.

Maybe it was the crowd of 15,569 that showed up to see the minor league team last Saturday night. A game after the Hawks looked sloppy and out of shape in their post-lockout opener in Detroit. They're still 0 for 1995 after blowing Monday night's game in Winnipeg.

Maybe it was the Wolves ad campaign during the lockout. The one about introducing a novel concept – actual games. Maybe it was that the Wolves have put those actual games on home TV this year. Maybe it's that the Wolves wanted to offer Sports Channel more games, but people there and other places say, "The Hawks sat on the cable guy, so they wouldn't show the Wolves anymore than their contract called for."

Then again, maybe Messmer had his own reasons for quitting one of the signature events in Chicago sports. Maybe his throat simply couldn't take it regularly, even if The Star Spangled Banner is about overcoming such things. How could he sing at every Hawks game, but

199

only selected Wolves games? As much as he's part of the fabric of a Hawks game, he's drawing a bigger paycheck as Executive VP for the Wolves. Yeah, money doesn't just talk, it sings too.

Maybe Messmer heard the lousy acoustics in the United Center. Maybe Messmer just wanted to come back to play the big room one last time, just to show that he could do it. "Closure" would be his word. Whatever, the whole thing stinks. After nearly four months of the NHL's greed fest 1994, we should be saying hello to the United Center. But after 13 years of doing a great job on the worst song, dammit, we're saying goodbye "and the home of the brave."

'Hawks Home Opener Has It All: Light Show, Messmer And Victory

--The Chicago Tribune

"Accept the challenges, so that you may feel the exhilaration of victory."
--Gen. George S. Patton

Messmer Confronts Shooting's Aftermath

--The Chicago Sun-Times

"No one can make you feel inferior without your consent."
--Eleanor Roosevelt

Chapter 17
A Journey of Faith

It was a rarity. A blank page in my appointment book without any major commitments for the day. This was partially by design. It was early June 1999, more than five years after I had survived the shooting. Things had, in many ways, returned to normal. I was speaking on a regular basis and singing, albeit with some lingering ill effects. But I was still feeling that there was unfinished business.

My career had evolved to the point where Kathleen and I were singing together again. I had sung at every Chicago Wolves hockey game since the night of my return, many of them performed as a duet with Kathleen. The Blackhawks association was now just a fond part of my past after completing the one final appearance in January 1995 of the lockout-shortened season.

My relationship as the Anthem soloist for the Cubs was still very healthy. I had even been flattered to have my voice become a permanent fixture for the millions of visitors to hear at Chicago's O'Hare Airport. A recording of my voice singing the Star Spangled Banner would now play continuously on the Chicago Wolves Level 6 of the airport's short-term parking lot, identified with my name alongside the team logo. It helped to remind drivers of the location of their parking spot.

Things seemed that they were normal again, but there was still something that had to be done. Over the time that had passed, I had worked through all of the anger, resentment and pain. I'd forced myself to confront my feelings. How would I act or what would I say to my assailants should the opportunity be presented to see one or both of them again? The questions lingered somewhere just beneath the surface of my outwardly positive appearance. My thoughts had often focused on the two young men that had since passed through their teen years and into manhood while incarcerated. Was I still unwilling to let go, or had I truly faced the difficult issue of forgiveness enough to move on with my life?

Repeated attempts to contact the young man who had shot me had failed. I had written a request to talk with him, only to be denied on one occasion and not acknowledged on another. In spite of my frustration, I believed that I had reached a point whereby I could honestly say that I had forgiven these young men. In doing so, over a period of contemplative and reflective prayer and meditation, I was confident that I had set myself free from the chains that had connected me to the incident. I was now concentrating on seeing the face of the man whose image lives vividly in my mind ever since the moment of the shooting.

I felt that this meeting had great importance to both of us. Somehow, I knew that this was to be the day to bring the two people together that had been indelibly fused by this unfortunate tragedy years earlier. The idea of facing my attacker was not something I was taking lightly. To prepare for the visit, I gave considerable thought to the conversation which might ensue, should I ever meet him face to face.

Starting the morning with a quiet and rather peaceful Mass at my parish church, I gave some additional thought to actually looking into the eyes of the only individual I had seen during the incident on that fateful night of April 9, 1994. I recalled the look on his face as I drove past him, both of us in varying states of shock. I remembered his expression of shattered hope from the courtroom in Chicago on two occasions: the conclusion of his jury trial and the day of his sentencing.

After Mass, I spoke to a young friend and briefly mentioned my prospective plans for the day. He immediately offered support in favor of the idea. It was an almost 450-mile round trip which I was facing to the Hill Correctional Center in Galesburg, Illinois. I knew it was a journey I had to make.

After collecting a few CDs, a roadmap and a large cup of coffee, I started the trip that was a journey of faith. My emotions were put on hold. What was the purpose of the visit? Did I want to confront this young man? Was my intention to force him into an apology? I had spoken so frequently already about the very topic of forgiveness and now it was staring me in the face. I thought it probably should have come easier than it did. I was still uncertain of whether true forgiveness had taken place in my mind and my heart or whether time had simply allowed the wounds to heal, both literally and figuratively. It would become obvious soon enough.

Naturally, getting out of the city was an adventure. Traffic, congestion and construction made the first leg of the trip almost taxing enough to make me turn around. Instead, I forged ahead, knowing that the open space and the country air would ultimately be welcomed. Surprisingly, I did not dwell on the events of my shooting. Instead, I found myself thinking about the person I was visiting. What was his state of mind? Had he become bitter as a result of his confinement and the culture in which he now exists? "Maybe the whole idea of the visit was wrong," I thought.

It was to be an unannounced meeting, so there was no guarantee that it would even happen. I might have been investing over three hours of driving time for nothing. But I took a gamble and the chance of gaining something positive this day was worth testing the odds. It might certainly be a test of faith. If so, I was prepared to face it.

Treating myself to the scenic route from Chicago to Galesburg, I allowed my mind to wander toward the words of Psalm 118, which had become my unofficial anthem in the days and years after my shooting. *This is the day the Lord has made. Rejoice and be glad in it.* It was a spectacular late spring morning, filled with sunshine, fresh air, rolling green hills and sparkling waters of the rivers of Illinois. I soaked it all in, knowing that the young man I was going to see had been taken out of this world and would have only a distant memory of the beauty that was freely unveiling itself to me as I sped west.

A road sign ahead read, "Galesburg 33 miles." The thought of my destination gave me a cold chill. I was too far to turn back now. At long last and in the snap of a finger, I reached the city limits. I stopped for gas on the outskirts of town and asked a local attendant for directions to Corpus Christi Catholic Church, a side trip I had planned. I was curious to see the displayed body of St. Crescent, a young child who had been martyred for his faith. The uncorrupted body was entombed within a glass display case inside the church.

I arrived just in time for noon Mass. I had not expected to be able to attend another Mass that day, but I welcomed the chance to delay my visit. As I entered the spacious and moderately decorated place of worship, I immediately felt welcome. It was also a last chance to have a brief conversation with God about what was about to transpire. My prayers were for guidance, understanding, acceptance and, most importantly, forgiveness.

The priest who had no idea of who I was or why I was there or the fact that I was even there, chose that day to speak about forgiveness. He convinced me that the Holy Spirit was speaking through him when he called out a hymn with the title, "Whatsoever you do to the least of my people, then you do unto me." The fact that that title of the hymn was specific enough to provide a personal message from the Gospel of Matthew was already capturing my attention. But when it was coupled with the text, which reads, "When I was hungry, you gave me food. When I was homeless, you opened your door. When I was imprisoned, you visited me," I was almost moved to tears.

After a short examination of the young St. Crescent, I could not find any other diversion. It was time to go to the prison and get on with the agenda of the day. Located just outside of town, the facility houses men who have been placed under the same roof for the purpose of getting them away from society. The residents of Hill Correctional Center are individuals who have murdered, robbed, stolen, embezzled, beaten, cheated, lied and destroyed things, including numerous lives.

I walked in the front door and tried to appear as though I knew what to do. At the same time, I was hoping to stand out as a law-abiding citizen, who was not to be confused with the incarcerated population. Somehow, I think my cover was blown when I answered that I never before had visited a prisoner in the State of Illinois. I got the distinct impression that the prison guard knew the answer before asking the question.

I emptied my pockets of all contents, as I was instructed, took my locker key – locker number 13 – and my written pass and headed to the next set of secured doors. It was not the room I had envisioned it would be. In my mind, I had expected that it was going to be a room where I was safe from the bad guys, where guards armed with clubs would be prepared to take action if the prisoner acted up. Of course, I thought this would all be taking place behind a bulletproof glass window, just like in the movies.

I was wrong. The room I entered was a cafeteria with vending machines and lunch tables. It looked just like so many company lunchrooms where people gathered to have their sandwich and discuss the topics of the day. This place had some recognizable traits – like a soda machine, a couple of microwave ovens and rows of numbered plastic tables with attached seats.

Drifting into this unfamiliar environment, I handed the guard my slip of paper containing a couple of bits of information – the name of my inmate whom I was there to see and a statement disclosing my relationship with the prisoner. I noted that we were "acquaintances," which I suppose we were at the very least. The guard looked me over and spoke at me rather than to me. Without making eye contact or breaking his stoic expression, he said, "Take number eight," referring to a table in the middle of the room. It suddenly took on a less than appealing aroma from some processed chicken that had been overheated in the one functioning microwave oven. I sat, folded my hands and waited.

This continued for well over half an hour until a different guard, who had temporarily replaced the initial one, told me, "He's on his way." When I had signed in at the gate, the guard had told me that it was not unusual to take a long time for the inmates to get from their cells down to the visiting area. At that point, the guard also told me that the entire prison was on lockdown following the "stabbing of four or five guys" – he couldn't remember – a couple of weeks earlier. Lockdown meant that everyone was in their cell 24 hours a day, seven days a week until further notice.

It meant that the men were even more frustrated and restless than usual and would probably be pleased to have the monotony interrupted by a visit. I hoped this was the case. What would I say? What would my first words be to this person? I thought the best opening line would be, "Do you know who I am?" As it turned out moments later, it was a question I would not need to ask.

As the young man I was there to see entered the room, he handed the slip of paper to the guard who showed no reaction from his perched loft behind a desk on a stage-like riser. The next frame in the scene was nothing I could have anticipated and something I will never forget.

As I spotted this young man, he in turn surveyed the room to see if he might recognize his announced visitor. There I sat as the eye-witness victim of the crime. I was the man whose testimony was single-most responsible for putting him where he was. Of course, I knew it was his own actions that night that were the sole reason for his incarceration. My first impression was that he had matured. The last time I had seen him, he was a frightened 18-year-old in a Department of Corrections jumpsuit, being led of out of a Chicago courtroom by police officers. I was pleased to see that he did not carry the posture of a beaten man.

At first glance, I made the assessment that he looked as though he had not lost his spirit. I made eye contact as he noticed me, prompting an immediate reaction. His face seemed to brighten with a sense of recognition and surprise. It was a moment of discovery for us both. The ease with which he moved toward me considerably deluded some of the anxiety. I dispensed with the prepared question. He certainly knew who I was.

I moved to my second choice of words. I began by calling him by name and said, "I'm here to see how you're doing." His response was one of both surprise and delight as he said slowly and repeatedly, "I can't believe you're here. I can't believe you're here." My own disbelief had already been tested moments earlier as I sat there waiting for his arrival into the room. Yet somehow, in just a few seconds as we exchanged looks with each other, we knew there was a common ground upon which we could build a discussion.

The words would not be difficult in coming. I held out my hand when he walked toward table number eight. We shook hands and held our grip. Perhaps both of us, for one fleeing second, needed to touch our only physical link with the other person who could help us recall the last moments of that tragic nightmare we shared. Possibly, both of us wanted to enjoy the memory of the last moment of our innocence before this lamentable incident had invaded our lives.

As we sat down to our meeting, there was so much to ask, so much to say. I felt the need to tell him what the impact of the shooting had done on my life, my health and my family. I didn't expect sympathy from someone whose own life had also been transformed and interrupted by the same event, but I did feel the compulsion to be heard.

After he had gotten over the shock of the fact that I was sitting there in front of him, he became very quiet and said, "I just wrote you an eight-page letter." I reacted with my own surprise, curiously wondering what it was and what he had to say. Yet, knowing that I would rather hear his words spoken directly from him to me. Now we would have that opportunity.

"Like it or not," I began, "we are indelibly fused to each other for the rest of our lives because of what happened." I looked directly into his eyes as I continued with my first wave of thoughts. "Nothing that either of us might say here today can change things. I can't make it any better for you and it certainly can't get worse." I said. "So it would serve no purpose for either of us to be anything less than completely truthful. I just want to know what happened that night and why."

He leaned forward without pausing, with an almost anxious willingness to tell his story. His version was virtually identical to mine, with a few more details of the logistics and the development of the unforgettable night. Details to which I had not been privileged.

I pointed out to him that there were only three people on the face of the earth that truly knew what happened and I was the odd man out when it came to knowing the full story. I entered the scene after it was already in progress to assume a starring role in this real-life drama, without my prior knowledge. Without a great deal of encouragement, he began to speak with an animated excitement. There was so much he obviously felt he needed to say to me. He never had imagined that he would have the chance to say these carefully chosen words.

"I wasn't sure how you felt about me. Whether you hated me or whether you would even read my letter," he said. "Oh, man, there's so much. I don't know where to start." I just reached across the table, touched his forearm and said, "Just start at the beginning and tell me the story," I said quietly. "But tell the truth."

He went on to describe his relationship with his mother, his grandmother and his siblings. He told me how his faith had grown during his time in jail. He impressed me as an articulate young man whose dreams had been temporarily extinguished, but who had not been defeated. We mutually agreed that the tragic episode that had brought us together had been an extremely unfortunate interruption in both of our lives that refused to go away.

My orientation to the culture inside prison walls was based on television and films. I could only imagine the brutal nature of the environment into which I had entered. It seemed suddenly contradictory to the purpose to place individuals in need of societal rehabilitation into a restrictive enclave, consumed with rage, violence, anger, racism and hate. The very environments we would hope to keep them out of.

I imagined that this young man was now living in just such a world. It saddened me to think of anyone having to call this place home. "A lot of guys find religion in here," he told me. "Even some of the really bad guys kind of settle down after a while." I couldn't help but wonder: How could faith be kept alive in such a place as this?

While we concentrated on each other's words, there were other visits happening in the same room. Couples were holding hands, children with their sugar-coated cereal spread out on the table were snacking in between the words they exchanged with their prisoner fathers. I suspected a sense of embarrassment, along with a sense of bittersweet joy at the beginning and end of each family visit.

All of the other conversations were being conducted in blind silence, as far as I was concerned. Our discussion was focused on a five-minute period on a given night where we were in the wrong place at the wrong time together. Amazingly, as I glanced at the clock, I noticed that we had been talking for over two hours already. Where had the time gone? Did time move as quickly for him in his brief escape from the mundane day-to-day existence of being locked in a cage? I knew the answer to my rhetorical question, yet I found myself hoping that his hell was lessened by each subsequent moment we spent in conversation. "Don't be a fool," I silently told myself. "Everyone in here will try to convince you that he is innocent," I blurted out much to his amusement. "I know," he said with a sad realization of just

212

how difficult it would ultimately be to gather some empathy for his point of view.

He said he would like to make people understand that his involvement in the crime was less than had been portrayed during the trial and, subsequently, accepted as fact by the jury. We discussed the details of that night, the moments immediately prior to the shooting. He described his instinctive reaction to the sound of the gunshot. His description of the action brought back the chilling reality of the moment as he provided a vivid account.

It was at that point when he looked at me in all seriousness and said, "I lied on the stand." Speaking the words he needed to say in order to set his soul free, he continued, "I told the court that I wasn't there that night, but I can't lie about it to you." He continued, "I know that you knew I was lying because we looked at each other that night as you drove past me in your car after you were shot. We looked at each other just as we are looking at each other right now." His words carried with him a sense of release. They were the words of his reconciliation. He had spoken the truth.

I could understand the significance for him to finally be able to speak the words that had haunted him. They had to be spoken to me, the only person who could recognize his perjury. It had been his last chance statement from a desperate witness taking the stand in a futile effort to save himself from the fate into which he was to be sentenced.

Again, I avoided the temptation to confront rather than console and merely reached across the table once more and spoke what I hope were words of acceptance and forgiveness. "I know," I said. It occurred to me that should anyone have the right to hate this young man for his actions, it would be me. Yet I found that I had prepared for this encounter by recognizing the fact that the only suitable action I could take was that of forgiveness. I felt that it was important that I convey the message that despite his captivity, in an angry and hate-filled environment, not all the world was like that.

In a matter of a relatively brief time together, we were able to address his fears and his dreams. I was also able to express my own set of emotions that resulted from our own shared experience of a few years past. We seemed to have settled on a peaceful agreement. It was both comforting and tragic. Sitting before me was a young man who could have possibly saved himself from all of this, had he been advised and counseled differently. Simply by telling the truth from the beginning, he still would have certainly been implicated in the crime as an accomplice, yet his degree of involvement might have possibly spared him the severity of the sentence he received, which would keep him in prison for at least 10 years.

I kept thinking, "Why didn't he step forward and tell the story?" As he gave his explanation, I found his answer to be troublesome and complex. He had been an above average student at the high school in Louisville, KY where he had been sent by his mother to get him out of the gang-infested environment where he had grown up. He talked about how his high school experience had been positive for him. He claimed to have been a popular student who had been involved in a number of extra-curricular activities.

He went on to describe the day when the FBI arrived on campus to confront him with his involvement in the crime. "It was picture day at school and I was all set to have my yearbook picture taken," he said. "When I got there, the assistant principal grabbed me by the arm and took me to the principal's office. The principal knew me pretty well. He was standing there crying, saying, 'I can't believe it,' when they took me into the office," he said. "There were all these FBI guys and Louisville County Police in the room and they were all accusing me of things I didn't do, like getting the gun, sticking up other guys and, of course, the shooting," he said.

"The next thing I knew, I was getting off a plane in Chicago and people were shouting stuff at me. Hollering stuff like, 'I hope they fry you,' and, 'We're going to get you.'"

As for his trial, he was very candid about his disappointment with his legal counsel, whom he felt never allowed him to speak out in his own defense. This critical error in strategy was what landed him in the correctional center, from his point of view. Although, he did make a comment that recognized the fact that, above all else, it was his actions and his choices – not the system – that ultimately put him in prison. "No matter what happened in court, I know that I'm responsible for my actions," he said, referring to a lack of good judgment that could have saved him on the night of the crime.

It was at this point that I interjected what I hoped was a dose of reality. Calling him by name once again, I said I wished that I could snap my fingers and help make everything a little better. I told him, "I wish that I could go to the warden and maybe help you to explain your story, but it wouldn't change things. I sat through the same trial. So did a judge and a jury. The testimonies and the facts of the case speak for themselves and the minutes of the trial are there to tell the whole story. As they say, the case is closed."

I finished my thought with a statement that if I did have the ability and the power to make a wish come true, it would be that none of this had ever happened at all. I said, "And I'm very sorry for all of us that it did." Our meeting was now over. We had said the words to each other that we felt needed to be spoken. We had looked a beast squarely in the eye and had lived to talk about it. As we concluded our visit, I realized that we had not broken eye-contact, nor had we let loose of each other's hand for two-and-a-half hours.

He made a request that we have our picture taken. He produced a photo coupon for the guard on duty, only to be disappointed when he was told that the lockdown had also taken away the photo privileges. I had a feeling that our time had been well spent.

I told him that he needed to make a commitment to pursue his education We touched on the probability that he would not see freedom for at least another six years. "I'm grateful that you haven't allowed this place to kill your spirit," I said. "it's important that you continue to grow as a person, intellectually and spiritually so that when you do see freedom – you'll be prepared for it as a much better person coming out of this place than the one who went in."

He nodded silently. Now showing his emotions, he understood quite clearly that although we had talked about freedom and going home and moving on with our lives, only one of us would do so on this particular day. A final handshake put an end to this very powerful conversation.

The visit concluded with a short prayer and a repeat of the words, "I'm sorry." Both of us were sorry we had met under these circumstances. Both of us were sorry this tragedy had occurred. Both of us knew it would never completely go away for anyone who had been involved. Our paths may never cross again, but we had taken this opportunity to speak the truth. What is most important is that we were able to deal with the life-giving issue of forgiveness. I prayed that both of us had discovered some newfound freedom as a result of our meeting.

Retracing my steps out of the visiting room, it became very clear to me that each of us are surrounded in our own sense of reality, as a consequence of the many choices we've made in the course of our respective lives. With one last glance, I turned to slowly speak my final words. Calling him by name for the last time, I said, "I bid you peace." With that, I left him to return to his world, as I returned to mine.

Taking the first step outside the prison gate into the fresh summer air, I knew without a trace of doubt that it was indeed a great day to be alive.

Victim Of Shooting Comes Back Singing

-- The USA Today

"One moment in a man's life is a fact so stupendous as to take the luster out of all fiction."
--Ralph Waldo Emerson

Thankful Messmer Wows 'Em Again

--The Daily Herald

"Anything worth believing in, is worth fighting for."
--Wayne Messmer

About The Author

Wayne Messmer is a Certified Speaking Professional, (CSP), the highest earned designation of the National Speakers Association. He is also a professional member of NSA-Illinois, the Screen Actors Guild / American Federation of Television Artists (SAG/AFTRA).

As a sought-after Opening and Closing Keynote Speaker, Corporate MC, and singer, he shares his expertise along with his talents as a Master Storyteller to inspire and motivate audiences across the country.

He appears regularly on stage to carry a positive message of hope in times of change and courage under challenging conditions using a solid platform of the "3-F's" of Faith, Family and Friends.

Wayne is a native Chicagoan, who takes great pride in his hometown, by celebrating his upbringing as a "Chicago guy" with humorous stories of the notable and influential characters who have shaped his unique view of the world.

He holds a B.M.E., Bachelor of Music Education from Illinois Wesleyan University, an M.Ed., Master of Education in Guidance and Counseling from Loyola University Chicago and a Ph.D. Doctor of Philosophy in Psychology from LaSalle University. In addition, he has been awarded numerous Honorary Doctorate degrees.

Wayne and Kathleen Messmer live in the Chicago area and enjoy two grown daughters, three granddaughters and a grandson in their lives.

Messmer:
' I Will Never See Total Justice In This Case'

--The Daily Herald

"If the world operated on an eye-for-an-eye system of justice, before long, the entire world would be blind."
--Gandhi

'Close To A Miracle'
Now Hear This:
Wayne Messmer Is Back

--The Daily Southtown

"I know of no higher fortitude than stubbornness in the face of overwhelming odds"
--Louis Nizer

God Bless Wayne Messmer

--The Chicago Tribune

"The greatest voice ever, Holy Cow!
--HOF Broadcaster, Harry Caray

Wayne Messmer

Made in the USA
Monee, IL
08 June 2020

32748062R00135